Dropshipping Shopify 101 2020:

The Ultimate Guide to Making Money Online With E-Commerce Business Model Creating Passive Income, Financial Freedom, Finding Marketing Products To Sell Online.

ROBERT ZONE

Table of Contents

Dropshipping Shopify 101 #2020:

Introduction

Chapter 1   Understanding Dropshipping

Chapter 2   Setting Up A Successful Dropshipping Business

Chapter 3   Dropshipping ebay, Amazon and shopify

Chapter 4   Pros and Cons

Chapter 5   Tools That You Need for Your Store

Chapter 6   What Factors To Look At When Analyzing The Target Market

Chapter 7   Marketing

Chapter 8   Dealing With Your Competitors

Chapter 9   Establishing Your Brand Through A Marketing Plan

Conclusion

© **Copyright 2019 - All rights reserved.**

The content contained within this book may not be reproduced, duplicated or transmitted without direct written permission from the author or the publisher.

Under no circumstances will any blame or legal responsibility be held against the publisher, or author, for any damages, reparation, or monetary loss due to the information contained within this book. Either directly or indirectly.

Legal Notice:

This book is copyright protected. This book is only for personal use. You cannot amend, distribute, sell, use, quote or paraphrase any part, or the content within this book, without the consent of the author or publisher.

Disclaimer Notice:

Please note the information contained within this document is for educational and entertainment purposes only. All effort has been executed to present accurate, up to date, and reliable, complete information. No warranties of any kind are declared or implied. Readers acknowledge that the author is not engaging in the rendering of legal, financial, medical or professional advice. The content within this book has been derived from various sources. Please consult a licensed professional before attempting any techniques outlined in this book.

By reading this document, the reader agrees that under no circumstances is the author responsible for any losses, direct or indirect, which are incurred as a result of the use of information contained within this document, including, but not limited to, errors, omissions, or inaccuracies.

Introduction

Dropshipping is a business model where there is no need to maintain inventory, own a warehouse, store goods or even directly ship products to the customer. This is all done by a third-party called a supplier. The store owner simply makes the products available for purchase to customers at a marked-up price. Then, the seller forwards the customer information to the supplier, along with payment, when an order is made. The seller keeps the profit.

If you want to make money with drop-shipping, you'll need the right niche for your store and the right collection of products to offer. To find a successful niche, look at the best-selling categories on Amazon. When starting out, sell products that are already popular in that niche. Then, as your store's customer base grows you can include other products. If you don't wish to pick a niche, you can run a general store. This allows you to incorporate a variety of products and you won't need to worry about being able to incorporate a specific item into the theme of your store. The benefit of a niche store, however, is that it allows you to build a reputation, or brand, within your niche and this reliability can translate into a more loyal customer base.

To sell these products, you'll need a website to serve as a store. This can be created using WordPress or a Shopify theme even if you have no coding experience, You can easily outsource this step to a professional. This store will be your business headquarters, so it needs to be neat, professional, and easy to navigate. Your website's domain name should be the same as your store name, so take this into consideration when naming your store. The products should be listed with multiple professional looking images and keyword heavy product descriptions.

Drop-shipping is one of the cheapest ways to open an online business because it doesn't require investing in any inventory. You can start a drop-shipping store for less than $100, but turning that store into a passive income stream will require investment in outsourcing and automation.

There are also some downsides to drop-shipping. The products you are selling are representing you, but you don't really get much control over what that representation looks like. Your store has no choice over packaging or presentation, although some suppliers might let you customize these things for a fee. Because you are the face of the product and the retail process, you are also held responsible if anything goes wrong with the product or the shipping. You'll have to be the liaison between the customer and the supplier, which is one of the reasons it's very important to choose the right supplier. You also have to go through the supplier if you need to contact the shipping company, which can be frustrating and time consuming. Over all, there are risks involved but drop-shipping can be a great introduction to online business and can provide a buildable source of passive income.

Chapter 1
Understanding Dropshipping

If you have ever thought in your wildest thoughts that you could make a difference in this world, you are right. You can be as successful as the leading millionaires in the world. Dropshipping is the one business opportunity that gives you a chance to rise above all your fears and discouragements. Even if you have tried business and failed a million times, there is nothing to fear in dropshipping. With dropshipping, you invest nothing, so you have nothing to lose.

What Is Dropshipping

Dropshipping is a type of retail business where the merchant does not have to hold products, store products or fulfill orders. In other words, if you are the merchant, you will not need to have a physical store for your products, you will not need a warehouse for your products and you will never be required to deliver the products to the buyer. This may sound absurd but it is true. Dropshipping is the only type of business in the world where you can sell a product you do not hold. You can sell the product and deliver it to the buyer without ever getting in contact with the product.

As a dropshipper, your work is to link the product buyer and the product seller. Now, this may sound like broking or affiliate marketing. Before you jump off the ship, first understand the concept. Dropshipping is a business; it is not an online marketing scheme. Dropshipping is different from MLM or affiliate marketing. If you have spent so much time or money in MLM schemes you might be a bit skeptical with online business models. With dropshipping, there is nothing fishy. Actually, as a dropshipper, you are in full control of your business. You are responsible for creating your business and branding it. A dropshipping business does not involve selling products for a third party. In reality, every product you sell should be your choice.

Dropshipping is also a good venture because it does not need heavy investment to start. Given that it is an online business, you will only need a few dollars to set up your point of sale. Once you are set, you will be ready to start making money. However, before you get into the business, you need to understand the key principles and concepts. You should understand what we mean by product sourcing and niche research. You need to understand how to choose the right products and where to find them. You also need to know how to market your products.

Understanding Dropshipping

To understand the concept of dropshipping, we need to understand the value of the internet first. The internet creates a whole new virtual world. The coming of the internet has turned the world into a global village. Given that all people around the world can communicate and link with each other online, it has become easier for the world to trade. This means that there is a huge potential market in most parts of the world.

Now, the internet creates a virtual world with virtual people. This means that you can also create a virtual store with virtual products. In simple terms, although you interact with people on Facebook, you do not have to talk to them face to face to prove that they are real. In traditional retail, a customer had to interact with the seller face to face. However, with dropshipping the seller does not have to interact with the customer face to face. Through online communication channels, you can sell products to individuals you have never seen. You can sell the products by convincing online users that the product is beneficial to them. You need a language that will help you appeal to the feelings and desires of your online community.

Understanding the importance of an online connection is the only way to grasp the concept of dropshipping. First, you have to learn to interact with virtual individuals. You have to know that as much as you cannot talk to people face to face, the virtual communities are actually made up of real people and they also have needs.

In this global village, there are also virtual businesses. Although the business may not be in your country or your locality, they do exist. These businesses include manufacturers, suppliers, and retailers. If you want to get into dropshipping, you have to create a connection with these businesses. In traditional retailing, you had to contact a supplier and visit their premises to discuss agreements. On the contrary, dropshipping allows you to contact your supplier and make an agreement without ever meeting face to face.

In simple words, the internet gets rid of the need to meet face to face in order to do business. The consumer can buy a product from the retailer without the need to meet face to face. In the same way, a retailer can order products from the supplier without the need to meet face to face. So, how exactly do you know what kind of products you are buying from a person before meeting face to face?

Just like everything else is virtual in the internet world, so are the products. You can see and even feel a product in a virtual state. Product manufacturers and suppliers are able to show you the product through images, videos, and words. Product descriptions and images play an important role in the dropshipping business. Without product descriptions and images, it would be impossible to sell anything online. Thankfully, any type of product can be photographed and described. With the images and descriptions, you can imagine and visualize the product you are buying without having to see it or touch it. The ability to sell virtual products makes dropshipping possible.

An online store is a virtual product store. This product store is what we refer to as the point of sale. Your point of sale is an online platform where you list products. Each product is made up of product images and descriptions. When you list products to your store, potential buyers browse through the products and pick out the ones that they wish to buy.

In traditional retailing, this type of arrangement would not be possible. Traditionally, you had to provide the actual products in your store so that the buyers could look at them before purchasing it. However, with the online space, the buyers look at product images and descriptions to get the feeling of a product. The same case applies to you as the merchant. You do not have to hold the products from the suppliers. You do not need to have a warehouse where you store the products. In dropshipping, when an order s made it goes directly to the supplier, who then supplies the product to the customer.

There are four parties that make dropshipping possible.

- The supplier
- The merchant
- The consumer and the
- Dropshipping platform

The supplier is the business that is responsible for shipping products out to buyers. There are different types of suppliers in dropshipping. In most cases, suppliers are manufacturers or wholesalers. In other cases, a supplier might be a more established retail store. The supplier ensures that all the orders that are made to the merchant are fulfilled. It would be impossible to have a dropshipping business if you get the suppliers out of the picture.

The merchant or the retailer is the dropshipper. In this case, you are the merchant. As a dropshipper, your work is to look for a market. The supplier provides the products, you provide the market. Just like traditional retailers, the merchant creates a store where they sell products. Think of a big brand like Walmart; they do not produce any of the products they sell, yet they have managed to create a global brand. They retail products across the world due to their trademark name. The same case applies to dropshipping. You do not have to produce any products but you can create a brand name. You can be known for supplying certain products and attract a certain type of people. As a merchant, you have to think about the easiest way to attract customers who need your products. Once you have the customers, the rest of the work lies with the supplier.

The product consumer in this business model is just a consumer, like any other. In most cases, people who buy products from online stores buy them for personal use. However, since online products are way cheaper as compared to those sold in physical stores, it is common to sell products to retailers. As an online retailer, you may easily find retailers who buy products from your store in bulk for the purpose of reselling them.

The dropshipping platform is the most important aspect of your online business. As the dropshipper, it is important to ensure that your business enjoys a constant flow of customers. It is also your responsibility to ensure that your customers enjoy the right products. To be able to do all these, you need a reliable dropshipping platform. The platform links you to the suppliers and the consumers. The platform helps you find the right supplier and products. Some of the best dropshipping platforms will only help you with marketing tools. Marketing and analysis tools will help you find the right market and products.

Benefits of the Dropshipping Model

The dropshipping business model is among the most profitable and one with the least risk. It has more benefits and fewer disadvantages as compared to other businesses. Some of the key benefits include:

Low Startup Cost

One of the reasons why you should choose dropshipping is the fact that you do not need money to start the business. The main reason why people procrastinate business is that they lack money. Financial capacity dictates the type of business you start and the locality you setup your business. However, dropshipping is not limited by your financial situation. Even if you are a stay at home mum, you can start a dropshipping business with your pocket change. Some of the dropshipping platforms such as eBay allow you to start your business with zero investment.

Unlimited Market

The other reason why people procrastinate getting into business is the market. Some may say that they have the right product but cannot access the right market. If the right market is your problem, then think about dropshipping. Dropshipping allows you to target the exact group of people who may be interested in your products. Thankfully, dropshipping is not limited by geographic boundaries. Even if your target market is in a different country, you are free to start trading in that country.

Little Time Investment

You probably want to start your business while still maintaining your job. If you are afraid of the risk of quitting your job to get into business, dropshipping gives you the right opportunity. If you think that getting into business may affect your work or education, do not worry so much. With dropshipping, you will only need one or two hours per day to check through your store, respond to customer questions, and ensure that orders are fulfilled. Interestingly, you can manage your store on the road. You do not even need to stay in the same place to run it. If it turns out that you are too busy to manage the store, you can hire virtual store managers to take care of your business.

Unlimited Room for Growth

With dropshipping, you can earn as much as you wish. Nothing limits you to selling a single product or opening a single store. You can invest in as many products as you wish. After all, you are getting the products free of charge. You can play around with as many products as possible and try to find out which ones are profitable for you. You can expand your market reach at any time you feel like. There are no geographical or social limitations. If you are experiencing limitations in your country, why not move your business to another country. You can sell the same product in another geographical location without having to relocate from your country of residence.

Access to Unlimited Products

It does not matter the type of products you wish to sell. When it comes to dropshipping, you can sell any product anywhere in the world. When you use a certain dropshipping platform, you are linked with product manufacturers and suppliers from across the world. These giant manufacturers allow you to pick any product you wish to sell. It does not matter your area of specialization. You can pick any product as long as you are convinced that you have the right market for it.

Access to Affordable Marketing

Another big problem for most startups is the cost of marketing. It is very difficult for SMEs to compete with established brands based on the fact that big brands have the financial capacity to market. Established brands also enjoy a large market share since their brands are already known. However, when it comes to dropshipping, every business has a chance. The online market gives you access to billions of potential customers. Digital advertisement is the cheapest form of advertisement and it is the one with the highest ROI. You do not have to invest in expensive print media or screenplay advertisements. With simple techniques such as social media marketing, you can grow your brand and start making thousands of dollars.

High-Profit Margins

Dropshipping being an online business offers the highest profit margins. The profit margins allow you to set competitive prices for your products. Given that you do not have to undergo the cost of storage, inventory management or product transportation as it is the vase with physical retail stores, you have a lot of room to play with your profits. You will realize that most suppliers sell their products at ridiculously low prices. When you choose to have your products sold online, you have a huge profit margin. Some products give you as much as 1000% profit compared to the standard retail prices.

Limited Legal Restrictions

Another big problem that most businesses have to face in the real world is legal restrictions. The process of starting a business in most countries is complicated. You have to through a lot of paperwork and approvals. Before you are allowed to set up your business, you are forced to spend a lot of money on a venture you are not even sure that will be successful.

On the contrary, dropshipping does not require you to go through such problems. If you want to start your business, you can start even without fulfilling the conventional requirements. Many countries do not have a defined legal structure for setting up an online business. Even those that have clear structures, do not have a clear enforcement strategy. Given that the online business world is so expansive, only a few countries pay attention to online business. With that said, there are some countries that many place restrictions on dropshipping. If you realize that trading in your country is a problem, you may choose to start an online store in another country. No one limits you to a certain location. You are not limited to selling n your locality or to operate from your country.

How to Start Your Own Dropshipping Business

You are probably thinking about starting your own dropshipping business and you are wondering where do you start from. It is good that you are thinking about it. The first step to starting a dropshipping business is conceptualizing it. Before you even think about venturing into the field you have to get a clear concept. I will introduce you to some hard facts that you must consider. While dropshipping is a business that is open and one that guarantees success, you also have to very careful when getting into it. If you start your business and end up a failure, you might never gain the courage to start again. This guide is not only supposed to help you start your business but it is aimed at helping you start a successful dropshipping business.

According to Shopify, the leading dropshipping platform, 99% of all new dropshipping stores opened on the platform do not succeed. Now, these are some hard facts to swallow. Before you dismiss this business model, get the facts right. Although only 1% of the business succeeds, all the business that succeed go on to make a six-figure income. Dropshipping is the proverbial case of one hot guy having a thousand girls while plenty of average guys struggle to chase one girl. It is important to note that, there is no shortage of market or shortage of products in dropshipping. The only reason why most businesses fail is that there is a lack of strategy. Given that starting a dropshipping business is free of charge, most people only start online stores with a trial mentality. People start online stores thinking that there is nothing to lose. As a result, most entrepreneurs do not give their online business the seriousness it deserves.

Dropshipping is a business like any other. It is not just an alternative or an incase type of business. If you wish to make money from this business, you will make good money. We are talking about millions and not just pocket change. However, if you want to take this venture as a joke, it will slap you right back in the face. You must realize that given the business model allows every Tom Dick and Harry to start a store, the competition is high. Each product you chose to sell is already being sold out there. For you to succeed, you have to stand out. For you to attract the customers out there, you need to show them that your products are not just picked from another website and relisted. We will get into the deeper details of establishing your business as we progress. However, to help you start your business here is a simple step by step guide.

Step 1: Conceptualize Your Business

Before you start a business, you need to have a concept. Your concept should answer questions such as:

- Why do you want to start the business?
- What do you expect to gain from the business?
- Whom do you target to help with your business?
- What solution does your business offer?
- What should be the future of your business?

A business concept that will work is based on a problem solution approach. There is no business that is established without the aim of solving a problem. For your business to succeed, you must see a gap in a society and choose to close that gap. If you want to start a dropshipping business, first conceptualize it. Look at the people around you or those abroad. Try understanding the problems they face in receiving certain products and think about the best solution to that need. This way, you have a good starting point.

Step 2: Do Market Research

In the conceptualization stage, you only make your business plan based on your observations. However, before you start any business, you must do research to confirm your hypothesis. Research will help you determine the market potential. The research will help you know if your hypothesis is true and if the solution you wish to provide will take care of the problem. As we delve deeper, we will look at the available options in regards to market research.

Step 3: Create Your Products and Find a Supplier

Now that you are sure that there is a gap in the market, you need to create a product that will fulfill that gap. For instance, if you realize that there is a lack of good dresses for short ladies, you need to start creating a solution to that problem by providing dresses for short ladies. However, you also need to create a product that will feel unique and special. You need to make short ladies want to associate with your brand and not just any other brand that sells dresses for short ladies. In creating your product, you have to communicate with suppliers so that the short dresses may be customized to have a certain feeling. According to your market research, you will find out what is the biggest problem affecting the short ladies dressing industry. Maybe, they only lack official dresses. Let your dresses for short ladies have an official feeling in that case. What if the dresses could be designed to make the ladies feel a bit taller than they are? It is such a minor factor that will make your business stand out from every other business out there.

Step:4 Choose and Set up Your Point of Sale

After creating the right product for your business, you need to start selling it. The only way to sell is by creating an online store. To create an online store, you have to choose the right platform. There are many factors to consider when setting up your point of sale. As we will see in the following chapters, each dropshipping platform has its ups and downs. The important point to note is that each option gives you a chance to sell your products. After deciding on the platform, you want to use, design your store according to your target market preferences. In everything you do, it is important to always think about your target market. Dropshipping is all about fulfilling the market needs. You need to appeal to the emotional side of buyers so that they give you their money.

Step5: Market Your Products and Make Money

The last and most important step is making money. Dropshipping is only sweet if you are making money. You may set up your store and list products but before you taste the money, you will never see the value. Product and store marketing are very important factors in this business. Without the right marketing strategy, your efforts may be futile. As we delve deeper, we will give you tricks that will help you market your products to millions of people without even using a cent. This is the guaranteed way of making money.

Where Do You Start

It is common for most people who want to get into dropshipping to ask where exactly the starting point is. Understanding some of the key pillars of dropshipping should give you a rough idea of where to start. In the dropshipping world, the key pillars include the dropshipping platform and the suppliers. Without product suppliers, the business may not be possible. However, the starting point should be a marketing point. Even if you have the right products but lack the market you will never succeed in any dropshipping business.

The first concept should be inspired by your market. Your concept of whatever you wish to sell should be inspired by the conversations you have with your social media friends. Of course, social media is a major player in the dropshipping business. Without social media, dropshipping could just be a shadow of what it is today. According to Shopify, 85% of Shopify store owners market their products on social media. This means that social media should be your first point of research. Through social media, you should be able to find out the types of products people are looking for in certain localities. You start realizing the constrains that people go through trying to find certain products. Social media trends and conversations should help you understand the certain constraints that marginalized groups may face.

Another important aspect that may help you find inspiration is your own life experiences. Every person belongs to one or several groups of people. As a member of a certain group, you understand the needs of that group better. This is often the most successful starting point. You start from the known and move out to the unknown. For instance, if you have six toes, you represent a community of people with six toes. You know the trouble that such communities go through in their search for shoes. This could be a good starting point for your business idea. You can start your business based on your racial affiliation, your body size, your sexuality or your religious affiliation. You can start a business targeting your professional field, your transport needs or your health needs.

Once you find a certain area of life you associate with, move to the next step, which entails linking your social issues to the real market. In this case, you start mobilizing a market by creating social media content. You start attracting people who may be interested in that specific area. Although this is not a mandatory step, you need to do some social media mobilization to gauge the possible market reception of your products. Through social media mobilization, you may create social media groups or join groups that share similar problems. For instance, you will realize that there are Facebook groups for overweight people that enjoy millions of followers. Through such groups, you can start your market research. You can post questions and start conversations that will help you know how different people deal with their weight problems.

While engaging with the potential market, you should also be doing product research. Is there any product that can provide a long-lasting solution to the needs of these people? Using top B2B websites such as Alibaba, start researching on the available products. A simple search in the Alibaba search area will help you determine if there are reliable products. You will come across the top products and read through reviews to determine the ones that are ideal for your friends.

If you come across a product that looks ideal for your friends, you are in a position to start thinking about starting an online store. Now start by trying every platform possible. Get the necessary information on the available selling platforms such as Amazon, Shopify, and eBay. Look at the advantages of each and decide how you wish to market your products. Think about the future of your business and the prospects of making money. Through your marketing efforts, determine whether it is possible to make a lasting brand from a certain online platform even before you invest in it.

Mindset

Your mindset will play an important role in your success as a dropshipper. As already mentioned, 99% of new dropshipping businesses on Shopify do not succeed. Given that the platform boasts of 300, 000 successful stores, it means that people open stores every day. For you to succeed in dropshipping, you must have a strong mentality. If you are an individual who expects things to happen easily you may give up. If you are an individual who easily gives up, your business may not succeed. There are 5 types of mentality that describe successful dropshipping entrepreneurs

- Positive mentality
- Don't die mentality
- Go-getter mentality
- Limitless mentality
- Authentic Mentality

Positive Mentality

It is all about the positive aspects of life. A person who has a positive mentality does not look at the negative aspects of life. You need to focus on the positives to succeed in any type of business. Every business has challenges and discouragements. If you focus your mind on the challenges, you may never make a step in life. In the same way, dropshipping has its challenges. As you get into the business, you will meet store management issues that will require your mental strength. Choosing to be positive, hoping for the best and working to better your business will help you stand out among others.

Don't Die Mentality

Don't die is a type of mindset where you never give up. A person who has a don't die mentality works out in the toughest of all situations. If you are thinking about getting into any type of business, you must be ready to face the challenges that come your way head-on. Although the journey will not be easy, you should remain focused on your ultimate dream. The same case applies to dropshipping. The reason why most people fail is that they think dropshipping is a get rich quick scheme. Although dropshipping will give you money, it is not something you should get in with a faint heart. You should be prepared to do your job if you wish to make any money out of the business. Do not get into the business thinking that everything will run according to your plan. Actually, you have to put in some effort even before expecting any outcome.

Go-Getter Mentality

A go-getter mentality is the type of person who goes for whatever they want in life. In dropshipping, you must learn to go for the specific something you want. As mentioned, for you to get into this business, you must relate your needs and the needs of the people around you. A go-getter person is a person who does not settle for the status quo. If you see something is not right, you go out of your way to make it right. If you feel that your group or a certain group of people do not get what they deserve, you have to go out of your way to help them. You stand up and find a solution to problems. A go-getter person is an ideal candidate for dropshipping because the business is tough. As you think about the future of your business, you must go for whatever you want. You should be the one who determines the kind of products to sell in your store. You should be in a position to go out and find the right suppliers and pick quality products. With a go-getter mentality, you are in a position to push your brand forward and ensure that it reaches the place you are targeting.

Limitless Mentality

With the limitless mentality, you open your mind to the impossibility. A person who works with a limitless mentality has wild dreams. You should have wild dreams for your business. Dropshipping is not limited in terms of geographical reach. For this reason, you must allow your business to thrive beyond the geographical region. You should allow yourself to get into the business and thrive beyond the borders of your country or your locality. With a limitless mentality, you are able to try out different types of products. You are not afraid to try out new suppliers and introduce foreign products to your market. The limitless mentality allows you to be the leader in your niche. You become the person that other businesses look up to know what to do. You set trends and go ahead of others by introducing products that others are afraid to try out.

Authentic Mentality

An authentic mentality is a type of thinking where a person values originality. The reason why most businesses fail in dropshipping is lack of originality. As an entrepreneur, you need to be original in your ideas. Do not just copy the ideas of other people and use them to run your business. You should choose products that are original in nature. The way you package your products should also reflect originality. You should come up with your unique product ideas and collaborate with suppliers to introduce products that are unique to the market. You should choose a unique niche if you wish to succeed. Most of the niches are already saturated. However, if you are wise enough to select a unique niche, you will be able to create a long-lasting business. The originality of your idea determines how lasting the business will be. Trying to build your brand on the ideas of other businesses will not help you stay in business for long. You need to open your mind up and spot original ideas. You need to look at the available market opportunities and utilize the gaps in the market. Without originality, your products will just be like any other product out there.

It is important to ensure that you are psychologically prepared even before you start thinking about the dropshipping business. Psychological preparedness means that you should make up your mind about getting into the business. You should make up your mind that you want to do business and that you want to do it the right way. Although you may not have as much money to invest in the business, a positive mentality is better than any amount of money. You may have so much money to invest in a business but lacking a positive mentality may cost you dearly.

Chapter 2

Setting Up A Successful Dropshipping Business

Establish A Niche

What you choose to sell is critical to whether or not your dropshipping business will last longer than a few months.

You see, consumers often follow trends, and that means you need to be able to follow trends as well with your business so that you can keep the profits rolling in. Trends are always changing, so that is why you need to stay on top of it. Luckily, even though the internet is part of what makes the trends fluctuate so often, it also now makes it easier than ever to keep track of them.

Thanks to the internet you can research the worth of a niche and whether it can bring you profit overtime or not. Don't eagerly jump on the bandwagon of a popular niche because they can quickly become oversaturated, meaning many businesses are trying to focus on that niche at once so that you are less likely to make money on it.

This can make the process of establishing a niche quite confusing for people just starting out since the basic idea of sell what's popular doesn't quite work. By the end, you will one hundred percent know how to choose and establish the niche of your choice.

Establishing your chosen niche can really end up slowing your roll, no matter how excited you are to begin. That's because it isn't as simple as we would like it to be.

You will need to sit down and truly brainstorm a good niche. Finding something you are passionate about is definitely an excellent start, but it is much more than just that. Then you have to focus on ideas surrounding that niche that could not only work for you but work with the current market.

It isn't as hard as you might believe to research a niche. You can start with what you enjoy, what your family and friends enjoy, and move forward from there. It all just takes consideration on what you can find around you and what you might be able to sell. Be realistic most of all.

Then once you have a few ideas, not just one, you have to research them all and then compare them to one another. You'll have the weigh the risks and the benefits of this niche and maybe set up a few simple plan models for each one to see what might work best.

Are you starting to feel the thrill of all this information? That's great because we are really going to detail the process now so that you completely understand and will soon be able to do it for yourself. Be ready to absorb it all and prepare yourself for the success that you deserve.

Niche Evaluation And Validation

A niche is meant to appeal to a specific audience, which means you can narrow down the types of products you have listed on your online store. Narrowing down to a specific niche can help attract customers because it can often be overwhelming to find a store that sells everything and anything.

Plus, someone looking for a specific product might end up quite confused if they click on your site and find all sorts of goods that don't have an obvious relation to one another. Your brand needs to be more focused so that the attention it receives is positive.

What you need to consider when evaluating a niche is whether or not it can fulfill the needs of your consumers. This means you need to think about the answers this product can give to those needs, the prices at which you can sell it, and the profitability overall.

To get an idea of whether or not a marketing opportunity is right for you, you can research the sales volume of that market. That includes checking out how often the items are searched and then see what type of sales volume you could potentially have.

Google is a great tool to use when evaluating a sales opportunity by utilizing their keyword tool, which is accessible and free to use.

The more specific you get with your keywords the easier it will be to see how popular it is and what type of traffic you can potentially receive for it. Instead of choosing a wide category you will end up focusing on a smaller category, considered a sub-category. This will lead to your overall niche.

Try and figure out the real audience of your niche so that you know who you are selling to, and see how that follows through with other companies.

Don't be afraid to use big businesses like Amazon to help you figure out what you are doing. You can see the levels of popularity on a product easily by starting to type the name in and see what Amazon auto-fills it with. That assists in naming your subcategories and validating what you are considering.

A dropshipping business is a great idea, but you have to really get to know your audience so that the products you end up selling match what they are buying. Your research should tell you whether or not your idea is worth pursuing, so buckle up and get to it.

Amazon uses a specific algorithm to do this auto-filling, so you can see that it would be a reliable resource. Be smart and use your competition to your advantage. It's not a bad thing to take notes from those big-name retailers, because they are who you are competing hardest again.

Starting to get the idea? That's wonderful because we are about to explore more about selecting, establishing, and resourcing the right niche for you.

How To Select A Niche

Finding a niche that you can sell in without having to spend a ton of revenue on ads is very important when you're starting out. If you are beginning a dropshipping business then you probably don't have a lot of capital to start with, so you need to be as thrifty as possible.

You don't have the ability to dive into whatever harebrained scheme you may have.

We've talked about the best ways to evaluate and/or validate a niche, so now we need to discuss the criteria for selecting one. If you have brainstormed a few different niches to research and evaluated them well, then you're ready to go about the process of selecting one.

Find the price point of items and seek out the most expensive that you can find. A good place to start would be eBay, but it's not the best place to take the prices of, Just use eBay as a general and basic guide to lead you toward products that could work for you.

It's not too hard to utilize eBay to help you in your quest to selecting a niche. Find a few products that are constantly sold in multiples every day and soon you can have a list of products that you know would sell for you.

Amazon is another great way to help you find items to sell. They have categories within categories within categories for you to explore, so make sure to do that. They have a wealth of items at various prices with plenty of reviews to sort through so that you can choose what you need.

Another important factor to take into account is not selling low-cost items. I know, I know, people are always looking for great deals, but you want to sell items that can net you a profit over time, especially since dropshipping is not immediately lucrative.

Alright, so maybe you've found a niche that can work for you and a set list of products that you could possibly sell. That's a fantastic start, but there are still a few more things you should do to help you select your niche.

Start looking for suppliers of these particular products and ask about their prices and shipping, and what sorts of deals, discounts, or availabilities they have. You don't want to pick a niche where the sellers already have established buyers, because then you won't be able to break into the market.

In fact, you usually make around 20% of the price of an item back. So if you're selling a $10 phone case you would likely only receive a $2 profit. The bigger your items are and the better-selling, the more profit you'll end up with. The math isn't too difficult.

You want to find those items that are more expensive but also sell well. Once you have a good set of those you are ready to get going.

How To Establish A Niche

Finding that perfect niche means that you are ready to establish the niche, but that can take a lot of work. Niches are not always the easiest to get going because it can be kind of confusing to figure out how to sell them overall. Often the niche is a subcategory that doesn't immediately spell out what you can begin selling.

For example, here is a list of 2019's top ten most profitable niches of 2019:

- Minimalist Luggage
- Home Gaming Setups
- High-Performance Workstation
- Home Gym Equipment
- Tiny Home Furnishings
- Custom Window Treatments
- Recreational Boating
- Home Theater Equipment
- Indoor Grow Rooms
- Kiteboarding Gear

These clearly are not niches that are simple to find profitable products for which shows how much work you really have to put into your niche to establish it. You need to know the market inside and out and have a lock on your competitors as well if you desire to make any leeway.

Make sure that you find the perfect name for your brand or store. You want it to be easy to remember and potentially unique. Stay away from anything integrating your name into, and make sure to remember that anything too long just won't be attractive to a buyer. Short and snappy is easy to remember.

One of the easiest ways to establish your brand is by utilizing Shopify, which is an e-commerce platform that makes it easy for you to set up your website and get started. You don't need to know any fancy jargon or hire someone else to work with Shopify, and it has multiple apps out there to help make shopping easy and stress-free.

Let's talk a little more about Shopify and how it can assist you when you are looking to set up your dropshipping business.

Shopify is the all-in-one that you need to get your business off the ground. Once you have that perfect name you can start working on that website, and Shopify is there to help you every step of the way with all sorts of helpful tools.

There are different themes, forms of analysis, and more on Shopify that make it easy for you to establish yourself in the niche of your choice.

You can also experiment with themes, styles, and more without throwing away a ton of money on a designer.

Shopify also offers apps like Oberlo that are a great help when you are setting up. You see, Oberlo is a great resource for amassing different products you may want to sell and is helpful when researching potential niches to choose as well.

It's lucky that these days there are plenty of ways to work on marketing yourself without having to hire any outside parties.

Ultimately, using the right marketing tools and ad selections can help bring attention and traffic to your new online store.

What Resources Do You Need?

Again, one of the most attractive parts of starting your own dropshipping business is how little it will cost. Most of the resources that you require are free to access, or at least inexpensive.

This, of course, includes Shopify and its attached Oberlo. They are indispensable when it comes to success at your new chosen profession.

This is because Shopify and Oberlo together make it easy for you to find products and add them to your store so that you can quickly become legitimate and get going.

Amazon, eBay, and Etsy are all also integral to the process of you finding the products you will end up selling because it is so simple to see what sells for them.

Google keyword analysis is another great resource to follow because it provides concrete information and numbers on searches. Market Samurai is a different product that utilizes Google's keyword process and can create lists for you to further research.

It is also important to establish yourself with a secure supplier so that your business does not suffer from the get-go with someone who is not reputable. Seriously, this is a very important step to take so be sure to do your homework properly when choosing who to work with.

A way to identify possible suppliers is by seeing what other sites use, such as Amazon, and see about partnering with them. Be sure that they can communicate effectively and have a resilient reputation so you don't end up in hot water.

If there is an issue with the product or their shipping they need to be able to respond back to you quickly and effectively, otherwise, you are just drawing out the issue with the customer which can lead to a bad review.

By choosing to work with established suppliers you are setting yourself up for more success. Even if it takes longer and you don't get the best deals it still works out in the long run for you because the reliability is so necessary when you are getting on your feet.

Utilizing the competition that exists is just as important when trying to establish yourself. You can order the same products from different competition to compare price, quality, and even packaging. This helps you get a feel for what the successful businesses are doing so that you can imitate.

Don't be afraid to see what others are doing because that's how you can take a full step forward, otherwise you are walking blindly. Even using the same suppliers means you can offer at a similar price range to your competition, that way you know you are just as likely to be considered when compared side by side.

Honestly, the possibilities are endless when it comes to your dropshipping business. It's up to you to use all these resources that are at your fingertips, just waiting to help you net that first profit.

Chapter 3
Dropshipping ebay, Amazon and shopify

How to Dropship on Amazon & eBay

If instead of creating your own website, you want to dropship on an existing platform or marketplace, Amazon and eBay should be among your top considerations. Let's discuss how you can set up your dropshipping store on these two marketplaces.

Amazon

Being the biggest name in retail e-commerce, Amazon has a lot of inherent advantages as a dropshipping platform. You can open a dropshipping account with Amazon and take advantage of their market share and stellar reputation to sell your products. Amazon buys products from suppliers in bulk, so they have massive inventory in warehouses in different parts of the world, which means that if you work with them, your small shop could grow fast and operate globally.

With Amazon, you also have access to a large market of more than 300 million users, which means that you could get large returns if you have great products and strategies. Because Amazon already has hundreds of millions of potential customers, you don't have to spend too much on advertising. In fact, you can easily advertise within the platform itself. If you optimize your page, you could get organic traffic there without needing to advertise.

Before you choose Amazon for your dropshipping platform, you should understand that they have one major downside. They prioritize merchants who use their FBA program over those who dropship with the help of third-party suppliers. If you are using Amazon's FBA program, you actually have to buy your inventory upfront and send it to Amazon's warehouses where it will be stored until it's shipped out to customers. If you wanted to limit your startup costs to almost zero, the FBA program probably isn't your best option, so stick with dropshipping. That being said, Amazon is a great place for drop-shippers because it has some of the best shipping times and quality control measures in the whole retail e-commerce business.

Many people think that dropshipping is against Amazon's terms of service, but it's actually not. Amazon doesn't allow arbitrage dropshipping (this is where people source products that are cheaper from places like Walmart and eBay and then sell them through Amazon). Amazon allows private third-party fulfillment of customer orders, as long as it's your business name that appears on all the purchase and shipping slips that are attached to the product. According to the Amazon TOS, you have to be the "seller of record," which means that if you use a competitor of Amazon's (like Target or Walmart), they may close your account.

Here is how to go about dropshipping on Amazon:

First, you should get a professional Amazon seller account. You should pay the fee for a pro account because the free account will limit your ability to grow and scale once you have started your dropshipping business. There are also certain categories in Amazon's platform in which you cannot sell products if your account is a free one.

You also need to get UPC codes (Universal Product Codes) for all your products. There are lots of services online that can help you acquire UPC codes, so with a little internet research, you can easily figure out how that works. You also need to get suppliers, and they shouldn't be big box suppliers (big companies that compete with Amazon in the retail market).

Use a product research tool to find a great product to sell on Amazon. Remember that with Amazon, it's even much harder to compete in popular niches because there are other sellers who have been around longer and they have positive reviews, so you have to go an extra mile in your product research.

You also need enough capital to sustain your business in the first few months because it takes a while for Amazon to pay its merchants, so you can't count on the payout from your sales to maintain cash flow.

Also, make sure that your suppliers ship the products pretty fast (preferably within 5 business days). That's because Amazon customers are accustomed to fast shipping, and the platform keeps metrics of its drop-shippers which customers can see. If your metrics are poor, customers won't be too keen on buying from you. Amazon is a bit strict when it comes to quality control, and if you get a high number of product returns or cancelations, or if your metrics are terrible, they could suspend you from their platform.

As a drop-shipper on Amazon, the way you create and organize your listings will determine how many sales you will be able to make. First, to increase your chances of success, make sure that you have lots of product listings on your account. Second, you have to be well organized in the way you list your products. Make sure that you use bold and clear titles and descriptions that sound like professional sales copy. You should also use high-quality product images for all items in your listings. As a drop-shipper, you may not be able to use PPC ads for your products because Amazon prioritizes FBA merchants over drop-shippers, so your best chance of boosting your visibility is by optimizing your product pages.

You should be careful when selecting the products to dropship on Amazon because not all products are suited to be drop-shipped on this platform. You should choose a niche where people are passionate and very specific about the products, which means that they will be willing to wait a little longer to receive that particular product. If you go to a niche where products are readily available everywhere else, you may not be able to compete with merchants who use FBA, mostly because of their faster shipping times.

Most Amazon drop-shippers eventually end up switching over to the FBA program. They use dropshipping to test the viability of a product in the market, and then if it works well, they switch to FBA to take advantage of Amazon's fast shipping, advertising, and other perks. If you have the capital, you can adapt this model to increase your competitiveness within the Amazon platform. If you would rather stick with dropshipping, you may be able to offer incentives to your customers to make them more willing to wait for a little longer for their packages. You can add a small freebie to every product that your customers purchase to entice them to select your products despite the longer shipping times.

Finally, when shipping with Amazon, be extremely careful about copyright and trademark issues because you could get authenticity claims from big companies, and Amazon could shut your down. Otherwise, Amazon is a great place to run a dropshipping business, and all you have to do to succeed there is to work smart and hard and follow the rules.

eBay

eBay is a great platform for dropshipping mostly because it adds a twist to the dropshipping model. Instead of just having a fixed price for your products, you can set up auctions for each listed item (especially if the products you are selling are rare and high-value items). It's also less restrictive when it comes to the kind of products that you can sell. Unlike Amazon, you don't have to worry too much about where you source your products, as long as you are able to deliver.

eBay is like the wild west of online retail because it allows people to sell all sorts of new and used items, so if you want to stand out and gain the trust of customers, you should be able to provide as much information about yourself and your product as you can and try to make your listings look professional. Compared to other platforms where you can start your dropshipping business, eBay is probably the cheapest because it doesn't charge any fees (like Shopify and Amazon).

To start dropshipping on eBay, go to their website and open an account. You can either open a personal or a business account, that doesn't matter since most dropshipping functions can be performed by both accounts, plus you may be able to upgrade a personal account into a business one if the need arises. The account opening process is fairly standard. You just have to fill in your personal information and contact information, and towards the end of the process, you will need to add a PayPal account to your eBay account. After signing up, you can personalize your account by adding a logo. The whole process should take you less than ten minutes if you have all your details ready.

When you start selling on eBay, you will only be allowed to list a few items at a go (about 10 items). As you make more sales, the platform will increase your limit more and more. You have to write good product descriptions with eye-catching titles for your products, indicate their prices, and then use high-quality images to show the product from multiple angles. eBay listings differ slightly from listing on personal websites or other platforms because you have to add terms of sales and shipping information within the description for each product.

For each product that you list on eBay, you have to go through the same listing process since eBay doesn't support synchronized settings across multiple listings. If you exceed your listing allowance, eBay might charge you a listing fee for the extra products. eBay listings usually expire after thirty days, so if you want yours to stay up beyond that period, you have to go to 'setting details' and set your preferred duration for that listing. The "Good till canceled" option ensures that your product stays on the site until you decide otherwise.

You will then input the price, quantity of items, payment options, buyer privacy setting, sales tax for the product, and your preferred return options. When it comes to returning options, you have to choose the length of the return window for the product, and the action that you will have to take when dealing with returns. If you feel like your customers could benefit from some further explanation of your return policy, there is a field where you can insert additional information.

You will then have to fill in all your shipping details. You can select different shipping options for different regions. You should also specify your shipping method, fees, durations, etc. You will then click the "list" button to publish your listing on eBay. In case you have left an important detail out, eBay will notify you and allow you to fix the error.

After you have listed your product, you could start promoting it on social media platforms almost immediately to drive traffic to your page. When you make sells, you will contact your supplier and have him ship the product to your customer within your stipulated time period.

Shopify

Shopify is by far the best online tool for drop-shippers who don't have the technical expertise to create their own shops. It makes it possible for anyone to sign up and start his own online store in just a few minutes. It's great for people who want to start a dropshipping business but lack the technical know-how or the resources to build their own e-commerce websites from scratch. If you want a hassle-free experience as you start your first store, you should seriously consider using Shopify. The service offers free trial periods for beginners who want to test the waters before making a financial commitment. Here is a step by step guide to help you start your first Shopify dropshipping store.

Choose a Name for Your Dropshipping Store

When creating a Shopify store, your first task will be to select a name for your dropshipping business. You want to make sure that the name you select is simple, creative, and memorable. If you already have a niche in mind, you could try to find a name that is related to that niche so that people can have an easy time figuring out what you are selling. There are some online business name generators that you could use to come up with a list of possible names before you narrow it down to one.

When you find a few possible names that you may want to use, you must check to see if they are available. Google each of your shortlisted business names to see if they are already in use. If you use obvious sounding names such as "American Watches," chances are someone has already thought of that, and they are already trading under that business name, so try to think outside the box.

Create a New Shopify Account

Shopify has made this step extremely easy. All you have to do is go to the Shopify homepage. At that page, you will find a field where you have to enter your email address to start the process. Once you have entered the address, click the "get started" button. You will then be asked to create a password and input your chosen store name. Shopify will ask you a few questions about how much experience you have had in the e-commerce sector, and then they will ask you to provide a few accurate personal details. After you are done providing those details, your account will be officially opened, and you can then proceed to optimize your settings.

Set Up Your Account and Add All Necessary Information

You have to go through your new account's settings one menu item at a time, and you are going to input the information you need to configure your account before it can be operational. You have to put in place the correct settings to allow you to receive customer payments, to create your shipping rates, and to establish your store policies.

When customizing your account, your first task will be to add one or more payment options to your store. Unless you have this in place, there will be no way for your customers to pay you for the products they'll purchase. Go to your Shopify settings page and click on the tab that has the word "payment" on it. You will have the option to add a PayPal account or to use other payment solutions.

We highly recommend that you use PayPal because it's extremely convenient and it has a deep market penetration, so most people who shop online already have PayPal accounts of their own. You can also opt for other payment systems if you find them convenient or necessary given the particular nature of your products (for example, if yours is a store that mostly sells products to offices and other businesses, you may find it more convenient to add a payment system that allows for bank transfers.

After you have all your payment channels in place, it's time to set your store policies. These policies will govern the relationship between you and your customers, so you should make sure that they are clearly stated and that they are compliant with the law.

Shopify understands exactly what kind of policies you might need for your store, so they have created a tool that enables you to automatically generate store policies that are standardized. You can immediately generate a refund policy, a privacy policy, and even a set of terms and conditions that will protect your store from legal liability in many foreseeable situations. To gain access to the policy creation tool, you have to click on the "checkout" tab, the go through the page to find each of the fields that you have to fill. You can then click on the "generate" button, and your policy will be set.

When your customers check out after making a purchase, the full text of the policy will appear, and they'll have to accept those terms and conditions before the sale goes through. If you have your own conditions that you want to include in the policy, there are some templates that you can use as guides to create your own policy.

Finally, you will have to declare your shipping rates. Many e-commerce experts recommend that you should account for the shipping price when you mark up the price of each item in the store, and then, you should offer your customers "free shipping." This is a marketing technique that works pretty well because it makes most customers believe that they are getting a great deal, so they'll be more inclined to go through with the purchase. You can click on the 'Shipping' button and select your preferred shipping options for different zones, starting with domestic ones and proceeding all the way to international zones.

Launch Your Dropshipping Store

After you are done with your settings and configurations, you should proceed to launch your new dropshipping store. To do this, click on the "sales channels" option, and then click on "Add sales channel." When you are done with that step, you will have a real online business that is up and running.

Design and Personalize Your Store

Now that you own an online store, it's time to personalize it. Here, you have to consider how you want your customers to view your site as they browse through it and make purchases. The design of your shop is going to be crucial, and it may have a huge bearing on your level of success as a drop-shipper. You want to make a good first impression when customers visit your site, and you want to project an image of professionalism. The two most important design aspects that you have to consider are the theme and the logo of your shop.

Shopify has a large collection of themes in their inbuilt theme store, so you don't have to worry about finding a theme that suits your brand. You can use a free theme option, or you can pay a little money for a premium theme. If you are working under a tight budget, a free theme will do just fine. However, if you are very particular about your branding, you may want to go for a premium theme. Try out a few themes before you settle on one. After selecting a theme, you can customize it to make it more reflective of your brand.

Logos are important for branding purposes because they enable customers to remember your dropshipping store in case they want to make more purchases in the future. Your logo should blend with other design aspects of your shop because you want to create a sense of uniformity.

You can use tools like the Oberlo Logo Maker to create a high-quality logo in a matter of minutes. All you have to do is play around with colors, fonts, and icons. If you are a skilled graphics designer, you can create your own logo and upload it onto your Shopify account. You can also hire graphic design experts for cheap on sites like Fiverr and Upwork. After you are done with both the logo and the design of your store, it's time to add your products.

Add Products to Your Store

To add a product to your shop, go to Shopify Admin and click on "Products." You should then click on the "Add a Product" button on the top right part of the page.

You will then have access to fields where you can enter the title and the description of your product. Fill the fields by either copying and pasting the text from your supplier's website or adding a description that you have prepared on your own. Make sure that you use colorful language in your product description because your customers are going to make purchase decisions based on that description.

You should then scroll down the page and find the "Images" section. Here, you have the option of adding images by uploading image files from your computer. You can also use "drag and drop" to achieve the same outcome. Make sure you upload your favorite product image first because it's the one that is going to act as a "featured image," meaning that it will appear prominently on the sales page when your customers scroll through your shop.

You should then review all your product details, particularly the "visibility" settings to make sure that your product is set to appear on the online store. You should also review the "Organization" settings and modify them to make sure your product is properly categorized according to Vendor, Product Type, and Collections.

You then have to input the price of the product. As you do that, you can select an option that makes it possible for customers to compare prices, and you can also check a box that allows a tax to be added to the final price of the product.

When you get to the inventory section, you should add your SKU, your Inventory Policy, and a Barcode. Indicate whether or not your product has a shipping price, then select the weight bracket of the product. If your product comes in different sizes and colors, you should fill the "Variants" section appropriately, and put in the different prices for each variant.

Finally, you should edit your Meta Title and Meta Description in order to improve your SEO (search engine optimization) so that customers will have an easier time finding your product online. Ensure that you save all your product information correctly and that you view your product listing from the front end to see it from the point of view of the customer. You should repeat all these steps to add more products, or you can use services such as Oberlo which can help you add products to your account automatically.

Start Selling and Cashing in

Now that everything is done, you can start making sales. Remember that dropshipping is a competitive business, so you should do everything that you can to promote your products on blogs, social media, and other websites. Advertising is also an option if you have the resources.

Chapter 4   Pros and Cons

The Advantages Of Starting A Dropshipping Business

There are many advantages of starting a dropshipping company, but in order to benefit from those advantages, make sure that you understand how the dropshipping model works and ensure that you stick to the model.

All retail businesses are inherently risky, but many of the risks of ordinary retail and e-commerce businesses are somewhat mitigated in the dropshipping model because they don't fall within your docket as a drop-shipper—most risks are borne by third-party suppliers. A lot of the advantages of the dropshipping stem from the fact that you as an entrepreneur are at liberty to try things out without having to risk too much.

Here are some of the major benefits of investing in a dropshipping business:

Less Startup Capital Investment Compared to Other Models

One of the most important advantages of dropshipping is that you can launch your business without needing to put down a lot of money into purchasing inventory. That means that pretty much anyone can start a dropshipping business. Even if you are a broke student or someone without access to much capital, you won't be locked out of this business.

In traditional retail businesses, before you are able to start your shop you have to spend thousands of dollars stocking up on inventory without any guarantee that you will be able to offload any of it. For most people, starting a traditional retail business would mean taking a bank loan, or using a huge chunk (if not all) of their savings on inventory. However, with dropshipping, if you are savvy enough, you could get your business off the ground with almost zero capital investment.

In dropshipping, you never have to purchase a product until you have made a sale, and the customer has already paid you. It's like being an agent who makes a commission by selling a supplier's product to a customer without having to put his own money down. In fact, when you are getting started, the only investment you absolutely have to make will go into setting up your online shop, registering with suppliers, and marketing your brand to increase visibility—none of your money has to go into production costs.

The agreements that people make with suppliers tend to vary, but the one constant is that you don't have to make an upfront payment for your products. If you find a supplier who insists that you pay for his product in bulk, you should know that he is not the right supplier for your dropshipping business, and you should keep looking around until you find one who is suitable for this model.

Low Overhead Costs

Apart from spending a lot of money on inventory, running a traditional retail business would require you to spend a fortune on overhead expenses, most of which you don't have to worry about if you decide to try out dropshipping. In traditional e-commerce businesses, you would have to rent offices, warehouses, and transportation vehicles. If you were importing your own products, you would have to pay ocean freight fees, and spend a lot of cash hiring warehouse workers to store, sort, package, and distribute your products. It would mean that you'd have to pay for rent, utilities, insurance costs, transportation costs, maintenance costs, etc.

Many traditional retail businesses fail because they end up buried in unforeseen overhead expenses. In dropshipping, you never have to worry about any of the logistical issues and the overhead expenses. You don't have to be concerned about paying warehouse workers, being late on utility bills or not being able to make enough for rent that month.

Most people run their dropshipping businesses from their homes (although if you find it necessary, you can rent a small office from which to run your operations).

Whenever you have an order to fulfill, you essentially outsource all the duties that are involved in the process to a third party, all at a bargained cost that is manageable. Your supplier will have to deal with storing your products in a warehouse, organizing and packaging the products before shipment, labeling them properly, shipping them, tracking them, and delivering them to your customers. The supplier will give you the tracking number for each product so that you can keep tabs on it, but you don't require many resources to do that. The only cost that is absolutely necessary, is the cost of operating a customer service line (preferably one that is toll-free).

Easy for You to Get Started

Starting a traditional e-commerce retail business requires a lot of technical know-how that just isn't necessary when it comes to dropshipping. When you run a dropshipping business, you don't have to spend a lot of time learning every single detail about how to operate and manage warehouses, how to hire warehouse employees, and how to provide them with a safe working environment. You never have to learn what goes into packing and shipping your products, let alone what goes into manufacturing them. You never have to learn the intricacies of optimal inventory management. You don't have to learn the accounting mathematics that goes into tracking products through different parts of the supply chain. All you have to do is find a reliable supplier who will do all of those things for you, and you will already be in business.

Can be Highly Scalable

If you run a traditional business, you would have to increase the amount of work that you had to do if the number of orders that you received was to increase significantly. However, with dropshipping, that doesn't have to be the case. The only work you have to do is to relay the shipping order from the customer to the manufacturer, so you won't be burdened with the responsibility of having to hire extra workers to increase your production. That means that once you have set up your dropshipping business to process a given number of orders every day, the only thing you have to do to scale up by any factor is to increase your capacity to receive and submit orders, which is neither difficult nor technical.

If your sales grow significantly, the only people you will need to hire to meet the increase in demand will be customer service people. A traditional retail business that finds itself in a similar situation will have to hire more warehouse workers, purchase more packaging materials, hire more managers, construct more facilities and warehouses, and invest more in transportation. In dropshipping, none of those things will stand in your way when you want to scale up.

Dropshipping is also highly scalable when you want to upgrade the quality of the product that you are selling. The effort that it takes to drop-ship an item that costs $1 is the same effort that it will take you to drop-ship an item that costs $1000. That means that if you want to switch from selling cheap items to expensive items, you won't have to exert any more effort than you already do. By contrast, if you wanted to switch from a cheaper product to a more expensive one in a traditional retail business, you would have to invest a lot of money into upgrading your production capacity. With dropshipping, nothing changes—you just relay the customers' orders to the suppliers as you have always done. If you want to scale up by adding new products to your online shop, all you have to do is find the right product and supplier, market test it, and add it to your shop.

An increase in the number of customer orders may cause you to run out of stock more often, but that is not a hindrance to scalability. If your customer base grows, you can always increase the number of suppliers that you have in order to meet the extra demand.

You Can Do It from Any Location

If you have a dropshipping business that is already operational, you have the flexibility to run it from pretty much anywhere you want, as long as you have an internet connection. The supplier will deal with every physical aspect of your business, leaving you to handle only the digital stuff, which doesn't restrict you to a given location. When you are setting up your business for the first time, you may need to stay grounded because you may have to acquire things like permits, a tax ID, licenses, etc. (some of these things can also be done online). However, the minute that you have all things set up, the only obligation you will have is to be able to stay in communication with your suppliers and your customers.

As part of your due diligence, while you are still establishing your business, you may have to visit your suppliers' facilities to verify that they indeed have the capacity to provide the product you are looking for on a consistent basis. However, beyond that, the business doesn't require you to be physically present at any one place. Some people have been able to operate profitable dropshipping businesses while on vacation in exotic locations, or while trotting around the globe.

If you choose to travel as you run your dropshipping business, you can easily communicate with your suppliers and customers through email. However, if you prefer talking to them over the phone, it's important to remember that international or cross-country phone calls can be rather expensive, and they may put a significant dent on your bottom-line.

Ensures a High Customer Lifetime Value

In business and marketing, the term "customer lifetime value" is used to refer to the amount of net profit that a business can generate thanks to its relationship with a particular customer throughout the remainder of his or her life. Dropshipping gives you the ability to increasingly expand your selection of products by adding new ones to your online store whenever you want to. This makes it possible for you to keep your customers interested enough so that they will want to return again and make other purchases in the future. This works best when you have found a niche that is unique, and you have curated a product line around that niche in a way that your competitors haven't been able to do.

Minimizes Your Risk

Traditional retail businesses come with lots of inherent risks, some of which cannot be mitigated against. If you put your money into traditional business, there is always the chance that your product won't move, and you will be stuck with useless inventory. If you operate your own warehouses, there are risks such as accidents, fires, water damage, among others. If you ship your own goods, there are risks of breakages, damages, and lost packages. When you run a dropshipping operation, you won't have to shoulder any of those risks.

If you are selling trendy products, there is always the possibility that trends will change, and people's tastes will be different in a few weeks or months. What if you sank all your capital into the inventory of that product? Well, with dropshipping, that is not something you ever have to worry about. Even if you invest in a certain niche product only to find out that its sales volumes are lower than you had expected, you can always pivot to another product without losing too much capital (your only loss will be the cash you put into creating your website and doing some marketing).

Enables You to Come to Market a lot Quicker

If you are familiar with the term "opportunity cost," you understand that any delays to get to market can technically be considered as loses. If there are two people looking to start e-commerce retail businesses, the one who chooses dropshipping will get started almost immediately, while the one who chooses a traditional e-commerce model will have to spend a lot of time looking for capital, learning the intricacies of the business and setting things up before he can finally enter the market. By the time the other guy official launches his business, the one who took the dropshipping route will already be making money.

Another aspect of this is how long it takes to ship products in traditional e-commerce versus how long it takes to do the same in dropshipping. In traditional e-commerce, you first have to ship the product from the supplier to your own facilities, then you have to ship the same product again from your warehouses to the client. It takes a lot more time for the product to reach the customer in traditional e-commerce than it does in dropshipping and that time difference matters a lot. If the product is a trendy one that could go out of fashion at any given time, the entrepreneur who chooses the dropshipping model will get into the market fast enough, make a killing, then get out before the trend changes. The other guy will get into the market a little much later, and he'd be stuck with outdated inventory if things change.

Sell an Unlimited Selection of Products

There is no limit to the variety of products that you can sell through the dropshipping model. You don't have to own or physically possess whatever you are selling. All you have to do is list it on your website or sales page to find out if there is anyone who is willing to buy it. That means that you can list as many products as you want, and you won't lose anything by doing that. On the other hand, traditional e-commerce retailers are limited to the selection of products that they already have in stock, and sometimes, they may have to hold off introducing new and trendy products because they need to clear inventory that is backlogged.

Because of the unlimited selection of products at your disposal, it's easy for you to expand into new markets. In fact, when some suppliers introduce new products, they will allow you to add them to your website for free if you are already in their roster of registered merchants.

Access to Unlimited Amounts of Inventory

There is no limit to the number of products that you can sell. If you have a good enough marketing campaign to go along with your dropshipping business, you may find yourself selling your products like hotcakes. If this happens, you never have to worry about running out of inventory because you are getting your supply directly from a supplier who keeps enough stock to service several merchants. Even if there is a likelihood that your supplier will run out, you always have the option of having backup suppliers. In theory, your inventory is virtually unlimited, so if you are well organized, you will never have to turn a customer away for any reason.

Less Time Consumed

Most of the things that you need to do to set up and to operate your dropshipping business can be done in a hassle-free and convenient way. You don't have to deal with the hassle of storing and packaging your products in preparation for shipment. All the labor-intensive parts of the job are handled by suppliers and wholesalers. You can also add new products to your sales page with just a few clicks and begin making money almost immediately. Compared to other retail models, dropshipping is indeed extremely convenient.

Fewer Products With Little Risk

All the time-consuming activities that are involved in the e-commerce retail process are delegated to other parties in the dropshipping model. The only thing you have to do on a day to day basis is to relay the customers' orders to the suppliers and send customers notification about the current location and the ETA of their packages. That means that you don't need to spend too much time running this type of business.

This business is, therefore, a good option not just for full-time entrepreneurs, but also for people who have other obligations. You can run a dropshipping business while you have a full-time job, a part-time job, or even as you pursue a college degree. If you have a startup e-commerce shop where you do your own packaging and shipping, your business will suffer if you split your attention and focus on other things such as a job or school.

Test Products with Little Risk

Dropshipping is the only e-commerce retail model where you can get to test the viability of different products in the market without risking too much of your capital. In fact, lots of experienced drop-shippers do exactly that. They list products on their websites and sales pages, and they wait to see if there is any market out there for those products. If after a while there is no visible enthusiasm for the product, they pull it off their list of offerings and try a different product altogether, until they find the one that generates the most profit. That kind of trial and error approach isn't a viable technique in any other model of e-commerce. If you put money into inventory that doesn't sell, you can say bye to your capital.

Increases Your Favorability with Wholesalers

Wholesalers love dropshipping businesses because they expand and boost their sales to levels that were previously unimaginable. Before dropshipping came along, obscure manufacturers and wholesalers had to rely on big stores and e-commerce websites alone to get their products to the consumer, and even then, it was hard for some of those products to receive any visibility online or even in physical stores. When dropshipping came along, it changed the game for wholesalers because they now have the ability to sell more goods and to reach wider customer bases.

Wholesalers look favorably upon dropshipping businesses, and some of them have been going out of their way to make their products and services available to drop-shippers. Dropshippers and wholesalers have relationships that are mutually beneficial, and if you start a dropshipping business, you too can benefit from those relationships.

The Disadvantages Of Starting A Dropshipping Business

Like many other business models, dropshipping has its share of disadvantages, most of which we will be discussing in this chapter. You have already seen some of the advantages of dropshipping, and as you read about the disadvantages, you will realize that some of them are direct results of the advantages that we discussed earlier. Some of the things that make dropshipping attractive to many merchants also have the effect of making it harder for individual merchants to succeed as drop-shippers. In other words, some of the positive incentives that attract people into these businesses have a way of turning into "perverse incentives" and ruining the viability of many dropshipping niches.

We are not discussing the disadvantages of dropshipping in order to scare you away from this model. Instead, we are outlining all the things that could go wrong with your dropshipping business so that you can know what to expect, and you can understand what you need to do to mitigate against any problems that may arise. We will be doing you a disservice if we only talked about the positive aspects of dropshipping without informing you about its negative aspects. If you fully understand common problems that drop-shippers face, you will be better equipped to distinguish yourself, to rise above the fray, and to succeed in your business.

Here are some of the disadvantages that you may have to deal with as you run your dropshipping business:

Low-Profit Margins

The biggest disadvantage that you would have to deal with in the dropshipping business is the low-profit margins. It's extremely easy to get started in this business and that has attracted many entrepreneurs, and it has made most niches very competitive. There are hundreds or even thousands of merchants who are willing to start online shops and to sell their products at a very small profit margin, so every new entrant into the game has to keep his or her prices close to those of everyone else in order to stay competitive.

The vast majority of dropshipping merchants build low-quality sites, and they barely offer any customer service, so their operating costs are low. When customers are looking for the product that you are selling, they now have online tools that will help them compare your product prices to those of other similar products, so even if you have a good marketing strategy, you have no choice but to set your prices low in order to make any sales.

The low-profit margin also results from the fact that drop-shippers don't get to purchase their product as a wholesale or "bulk" price because they sell their products one item at a time. Compared to a traditional e-commerce shop that carries its own inventory, drop-shippers have to pay more per item, so at the end of the day, their profit margins are limited.

Wholesalers are right to charge drop-shippers more than other merchants because they go through a lot of trouble to package each item individually rather than sending out bulk orders. This costs them more in terms of packaging material, labor, and transportation costs, so they feel the need to transfer those costs to the owner of the dropshipping business.

The profit that you make as a retailer in the dropshipping business is your selling price minus all other costs, including the cost of buying from the supplier, shipping costs, and your own operating costs (e.g. the amount you pay for ads and content development). If you already have less than a 20% margin to work with after subtracting the supplier's charge, you can end up with a really minuscule profit margin.

In order to make decent profits as a drop-shipper, you have to move high volumes of the product. You can also do a lot of research in order to identify a niche that works well with the dropshipping model. We will be discussing how to find a great niche later in this book.

Suppliers Are Prone to Making Human Errors

Dropshipping suppliers tend to service a lot of merchants, and because of the high volumes of the orders that they have to fulfill, they often end up making human errors. If you have chosen to work with the cheapest supplier as a way to cut your costs, chances are that he would end up making frequent mistakes in which the customers will end up blaming you because they are doing business with you, and not your supplier.

If the supplier fails to keep his stock levels up, you may end up accepting orders from customers only to find out that your supplier is unable to fulfill them. Whenever there are bungled shipments or missing packages, you will have no choice but to take responsibility for the errors. You can mitigate against some of the human errors by having backup suppliers and backups to the backups so that if one supplier fails, you don't have to let down your customer and come across as unprofessional.

Issues with Inventory

Compared to traditional e-commerce businesses that stock their own inventory, dropshipping means that you have no idea how much stock is actually available at any given time, so you have to source your products from multiple suppliers to avoid a scenario where you run out of stock. However, even that solution presents its own problems with your inventory. Some technological solutions are available to help owners of dropshipping businesses sync up their sales records with their suppliers' stock records, but most suppliers don't invest in support systems for such technologies because they aren't the primary benefactors of such technologies. Technological solutions also fall short because it's hard to project the suppliers' inventory depletion rate since they service multiple dropshipping businesses at the same time.

Shipping Costs Can Get Complicated

Many drop-shippers work with multiple suppliers at any given time, and this opens up the opportunity for shipping costs to get really complicated and unnecessarily high. Take the example of a customer who orders a handful of items from your dropshipping business. If you source each item from a different warehouse, you will have to pay a shipping fee for each of the items that the customer receives. You will have a difficult time convincing a customer who has checked out multiple items in one cart that there is a shipping cost attached to each individual item— customers who are used to shipping deals from places like Amazon may find that ridiculous. They'll assume you are trying to grossly overcharge them for shipping, and they may even decide not to buy your products anymore. If you choose to offset the shipping costs on your end, you may find yourself actually making a loss on that sale! In a scenario such as this one, it's impossible for you to come out on top.

Competition

Because it's easy to get started, there are many people who have set up dropshipping businesses, and while this is a good thing for the consumer, it is a very big challenge for you if you want to succeed as a drop-shipper. You can find that hundreds of people are selling the same exact product, so it makes it hard for anyone person to break out from the crowd and to make extraordinary amounts of profits. In many cases, you even have to go up against juggernauts like Walmart or Amazon who won't hesitate to undercut smaller retailers whenever they feel like it. When the profit margin is already low, you have very little room to outmaneuver dozens if not hundreds of competitors.

Shipping Can Be Slow

Marketing research shows that shipping time is one of the main factors that most online shoppers consider when they are looking to make a purchase decision. When you drop-ship your customers' orders, you don't have any control over the logistics of your shipments, which means that you can't optimize shipping times. You just have to rely on your supplier's shipping speed and hope that he always keeps it up. If you had a traditional e-commerce retail shop where you do your own shipping, you would be able to provide your customers with a lot more shipping options, and you would be able to offer them guarantees when it comes to delivery times.

Suppliers aren't particularly keen on going out of their way to make fast deliveries. Faster shipping times mean additional costs for suppliers, so they are contented to do the bare minimum. At the same time, giant retailers like Amazon are doing everything in their power to cut down their shipping times, so it makes it very hard for drop-shippers to compete. Even if a supplier offers tiered delivery services at different costs, as a drop-shipper, you may find it hard to select the fastest and most expensive package because it would affect your profit margin which is already small, to begin with.

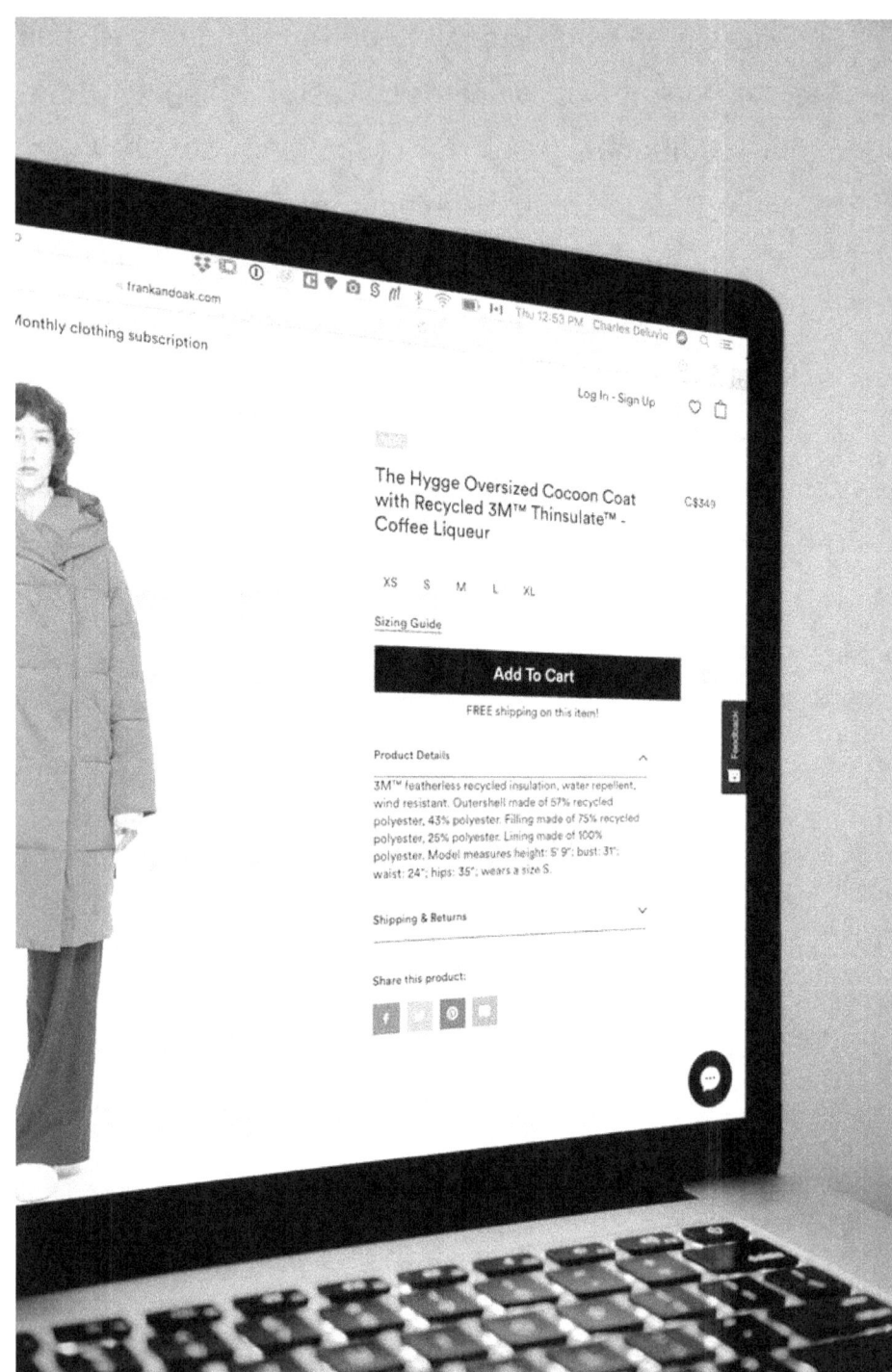

Chapter 5

Tools That You Need for Your Store

In this rapidly changing world, no business can survive without using certain online tools. These provide assurance to the business when trends change and act as a backbone whenever any support is required. The convenience that using an online tool provides is incomparable to other manual forms. Whether it is making calculations for inventory or to make business expansion plans, technology plays the biggest and most significant role. Productivity and efficiency have increased by a lot, especially in the past decade as businesses of all sizes have had the opportunity to update its online services. The constant need to be updated with changing technology is essential for businesses to be able to attract new customers with ease.

Creating your e-commerce store

To explore the potential of your store, you need to be ready to adapt to all the available platforms, which will ensure the sustainability of your business. Before even looking all of the options available to make your store stand out, creating an e-commerce store is the first step. It is a necessity to have sound knowledge in technology and the online tools that are out there to start. There are professionals who can set the store up for you, as well as websites solely dedicated to help out beginners like you. Do not hesitate to seek help! These platforms are very well suited to e-commerce entrepreneurs who are just starting out. Moreover, these applications can guide you through steps to manage almost everything when launching your store.

Picking a theme

Now comes the part where you need to focus on particular and intricate details of your niche that will define your e-commerce store. However, before this step, you need to have good knowledge of the type of products you want to work with. The very inspiration for having a relevant theme that portrays your vision comes from your product range. If you are seeking help from a professional website or application, you will find a lot of preset themes there already. These can help you in brainstorming ideas and making decisions if you are unsure where to start. More importantly, think about customizing your store and giving it a unique touch. In a lot of cases, generic designs can be a turn off to consumers, while innovative ones can entice high-end customers and turn them into returning customers in the long run.

Designing an e-commerce store

Whenever customers visit your store, the theme, color palette and the design are the first things that they notice. At times, you may wonder, "Why do I need to put an extra effort into making it pretty?" or "Isn't having a great range of products enough?" Well, the answer is simple - if consumers are not interested, they will not bother going through whatever your store has to offer. Having an aesthetically pleasing e-commerce store entices customers and also validates your business as a professional one. With word of mouth, more people can become aware of and take notice of your store. If it is unorganized or shabby, it would be very difficult for you to attract them. Hence, to have and maintain loyal and potential customers, investing your resources on building a good e-commerce store is a necessity.

Online Logo Makers

After you have designed and set your store up, now is the time to brand it. This helps to gain recognition for your products and creates a lasting first impression in the minds of the customers. It can be anything from a simple tree to an intricate design; this should depend on the type of products you are selling. It is better to be more open to ideas and new designs instead of being adamant on one. Having a professional store can do wonders and help create a buzz among customers. Hence, a logo is the simplest and best solution for you to put your business out there. If you want to experiment, do not shy away from creating your own design but if you are not proficient enough, do not shy away from help from online logo makers. Hiring graphic designers or outsourcing can be great options too, depending on the budget you have for creating the logo.

Payment processing

Due to globalization, we have access to faster services, much faster than those in the past. The systems for making online payments have developed immensely and have made it easier for us to make daily purchases. You do not need to carry cash around all the time. Their personal information and details are encrypted and have protection from credit card frauds for when businesses are willing to adopt such models. You should do research on the most common online methods of making payment among your targeted customers and make sure that you provide them with those payment services. PayPal is one of the most efficient systems in the most recent times. You can also be open towards offline payment services but the online payment methods are much more convenient in today's time.

Online business plan services

If you are happy with your strategies and find that they are working for your business, this should not be a tool you need. However, it is recommended that you explore these services. An outside perspective is necessary for you to be able to work on your shortcomings. For entrepreneurs, these online plans for your business guide you in designing a feasible and strong plan when you are making the transition from great idea to a profitable business venture. The inbuilt features and tool templates of web based applications help you generate charts on performance and goal achievement. Your financial status, depending on investments made for the business, can be studied carefully. You can be in charge of and keep track of the progress that you are making. Once you learn about what the services offer you, it would not be a surprise to see that you have started to think more critically and that your ideas for your store and product line go beyond the surface.

Using social media for your store

Whether you want to focus on Facebook, Instagram, Twitter, or any other social networking website, engagement with your customers through this platform is one of the most effective ways to draw and drive traffic to your store. Using social media is attractive as you do not have to invest a lot of money into it and you can utilize it to broaden your reach. Millions of people all around the world can engage with your store. Specialized tools on individual platforms are available to make social media users aware of new products and you have the flexibility to promote your products and content related to them. This also helps you to create a brand for your store. The best part is that as more time passes by, these platforms continue to grow and once you can get comfortable with social media, you should expect to look at great numbers!

Web hosting

The pace of the business world is much faster than what it was ten years ago. You cannot expect to apply those same strategies for attracting customers today. Hence, if you have not explored the internet yet, you will lag behind and before you realize, you will already be out of the game. A web hosting service allows you to start a website and run it. The files that makeup the website on a data server can be stored through these services and these files are uploaded to the web automatically from your web hosting service. The use of email marketing and installation of one-click supported applications are some of the many features that you can use when building your business. You can also be assigned an email address that includes the site's domain name.

Shopping cart software

When you have set up your website, there are some additional things which you need to offer your customers when they make a purchase. Shopping cart software is necessary to be able to make payments through your website. This is not only beneficial for the customers as it can allow them to feel safe when buying something online, but it is an advantage for your store too. Tracking inventory gets easier and you can keep tabs on which product to promote or communicate with the suppliers if a surge is predicted with the latest trends. This will also help you produce reports based on this data through your website's services. This software can be connected to multiple platforms for making payments. PayPal or credit card services can be offered to customers and this makes their experience more familiar as well. The purchasers can also be aware of the amount of tax they are paying and how much they are being charged for shipping costs. You promote transparency and convenience through these services on your store's website and it will help you gain a good reputation among old and new customers.

Webinar services

As your business grows, you may think of expanding and gaining new customers, both locally and internationally. Webinar services can help you connect and take orders faster and most importantly, they can help you monitor your day to day operations, especially if you have multiple offices. This will help you out if your employees are working remotely and if you have multiple working locations. Training sessions, meetings with all of your employees, either within a specific branch or all together, can be conducted much more comfortably. Webinar services are a great fit for you when you want to present your sales online and make product demonstrations for your clients too. Becoming more proficient in this helps you connect with your customers faster and you can respond to their queries in real time.

Anti-virus software

When you are using your computer, it is highly likely that you are storing information through a variety of applications. Whether you are dealing with storing personal information or you are processing orders, you need to keep all the data in an organized way. The information stored here is valuable and not having any protection programs on your computer puts you and your business in a lot of danger. Apart from the technical issues that your computer will go through, you could experience data theft, which would be a very big loss for your business venture. All businesses should have anti-virus software to guard the computer network against viruses, malware, Trojans, worms, or spyware. Since the platform of dropshipping is online where you have to constantly be in touch with your suppliers and customers, having a good antivirus software is a necessity and it is equally necessary for protection.

Receiving payments from customers

In order to deal with customers from various backgrounds, your knowledge in different modes of payment platforms is required. It reduces hassle if you can connect to multiple platforms that your customers will feel safe using. There are additional charges when you want to use these online payment platforms, ensuring to keep you safe against business fraud. You will be charged a fee for every sale you make and an additional amount to ensure protection for your store. You should check out different platforms apart from PayPal to make a sound decision, however, it is and has been the most trusted and convenient one in the market. Apart from this, there are built-in features to provide you protection if you are using platforms like Shopify.

Online data storage

Due to the ease of an online platform, storing data has become much easier than it used to be. Online data storage acts as backup storage if anything goes wrong with your computer. Of course, you can access your data online even if no problems arise instead of relying on your computer's storage. Data is stored on a cloud server which is convenient and safe. You can access the files from any part of the world at any time. Also, if you want to free up space on your computer, having online data storage is the best way to go about this. It is wiser to have online storage as hard drive failures, theft, and file erasure can occur and make these files extremely difficult to retrieve.

Business tools that you should know how to use
Google AdWords & Analytics

Google is the place we think of going instantly whenever there is something we want to know. From getting instant information about the most complicated technologies to doing the most basic spell checks, Google is our one-stop solution. For your business, you need to learn to make the most of this platform. Whenever you want to know about anything, this search engine can give you around 40,000 results per second and is definitely the most reliable search engine today. You can focus on getting on the first page of the search list and witness how this changes your income. Use an SEO (search engine optimization) strategy to try and make it on the first page. It may take a long time, maybe even months or longer, but you should keep at it. This will ensure you benefits in the long term. However, there is another way that can help you attain a first-page position faster, and this strategy includes using Google AdWords. This is a scheme of paid ads where you pay every time a visitor clicks on your advertisement. Additionally, you need to invest time into how to utilize Google Analytics and understand its importance for your website and your business. This tool allows you to understand the types of mediums through which your visitors come from and this could be a huge advantage when you are starting out or are struggling to reinvent your line. Overall, this will assist with things that are working and not working, guiding you towards better execution and expansion plans.

SurveyMonkey

Now that you have set your store up and are getting ready to attract customers to your niche, you need to know about the current market and what the trends are. This is a surveying tool available online that helps you connect with your audience. Survey Monkey already has a lot of preset questions along with built-in templates to give you a thorough insight when analyzing data. The best aspect is that the tool gives unbiased responses which can help you modify your strategies or help you create new and improved ones. The free version of this tool still provides you a lot of information through the surveys but the number of features is limited. Give it a try and see how much it helps improve your product line. If you are finding it useful, go ahead and get a subscription with a paid plan. The paid plan will provide many more useful tools for surveying.

X-Cart

For newcomers who do not have a lot of money to start out but want to give dropshipping a shot, your e-commerce website still needs to stand out. This tool is cost-effective and will not put a strain on your funds. X-Cart has a free version if you want to give it a try and see whether you find it suitable for your business or not. It helps you build your website and you can explore its various features. Moreover, free extensions will allow you to create shipping labels, slideshows, and do so much more! Your business can access these facilities and prioritize what will be more beneficial to get started on in terms of harnessing technical skills. You can get acquainted with the different themes available online and customize them wherever you feel necessary.

Tableau Public

This is a marketing tool that helps you to conduct research and lets you make a thorough analysis of your business data. You learn to make better predictions on what will work and what will not and this helps you make better decisions for the future. This tool is very effective because it sources out data from CSV files and Excel among many others. When the business venture is new, investing in high profile marketing research tools is important but expensive. This is where this tool is handiest as it can give free access to up to 15 million rows in one workbook and provide data solutions for free with up to 10 gigabytes of space.

BuzzSumo

In the modern day, social media has been the best platform for marketing. Social media is perfect for if you want to understand demographics, connect with influencers, find out what the most shared content is and much more. BuzzSumo is the best influencer marketing tool that allows you to find out what content is performing the best on any social media platform. You can choose a paid subscription but there is a free trial period too which you should definitely make use of before making a purchase. This application helps you understand what sort of content will work well with your product line; this in turn will help you connect with influencers who can help you in expanding your marketing strategies.

Designhill

Lack of personalization during the shipment process, executed by your suppliers can make it difficult for your customers to relate with your brand. In such a scenario, you can simply add your logo to the package; this will help you promote your brand. Through Designhill, you can access countless templates for free and it even helps you create your own brand name. You can insert your store's name and pick themes, colors, icons to match your niche. You can choose a logo from the app's generated logos and purchase it to obtain the copyright. You can spend according to your budget and get started with this graphic design platform. The platform is powered by AI and allows you to design a logo on the go.

These tools should give you an idea about the factors that are important for you to be updated on to run your business smoothly. You should focus on your niche and work around it with the insight of technology. Since technology improves every day, it is useful to become proficient at using these applications as you gain more experience through your dropshipping store. It will help you explore better solutions to your needs and gain technical expertise accordingly.

Chapter 6
What Factors To Look At When Analyzing The Target Market

Demographics

Demographics is a term that relies to certain data about people, such as where they are located, i.e. their geographic location, as well as what income bracket they belong to, and other such information. Being able to gather this data and use it to define a particular market is crucial to understanding just how large your target market really is and where they are centered around, and will be extremely useful in catering the product catalog to their demand.

Gender

One of the undeniable and statistically observed differences between genders is the general shopping and spending patterns between men and women, as men and women have varying shopping patterns when purchasing things, whether online or in a physical store. Gender is not the most controlling factor when deciding on a target market, but it still offers insight that may be useful when targeting a particular market segment. Some things that can be influenced by gender is the type of content that motivates them to buy, what language to use in write – ups to make products more attractive, or even what times of day they tend to shop, all these are factors that may be influenced by gender.

Age

Age is a major factor in deciding a person's spending and purchasing pattern, especially due to the change in tastes over generations, as well as the general difference in spending capacity depending on age. For example, millennials, the nickname given to the demographic group born in the last 2 decades of the 1900's, tend to do a lot of shopping online, but due to the relative youth of this group, have a lower spending capacity and thus rarely spend on big – ticket items online. Another example would be those in the ages of sixty and above, who are generally more unfamiliar with ecommerce and are not as comfortable shopping online, and thus are less likely to buy things through the internet.

Institution

One thing to keep in mind is what type of sales you will be making, if these products will be sold directly to consumers, to other businesses, or even to government institutions. Whether these goods are being sold Business – to – Consumers (B 2 C), business – to – business (B 2 B), or Business – to – government (B 2 G) are all factors in deciding many aspects of the business, such as what types of product should be offered, how many products they will be purchasing, and how these products and services will be marketed. However, most drop shipping businesses sell directly to consumers, using the B2C relation, but in the case that the retailer's drop shipping business will also cater to other institutions, these factors should be taken into account.

Know the Competition

Earlier we discussed how checking up on competitors is a part of market research. This aspect cannot be emphasized enough, as in order to beat the competition, one needs to know them well. For example, if the product that the retailer or merchant wishes to sell is already being sold at a high volume by established and well – known online retailers, then this is a positive sign for the retailer. However, if the retailer notices that that very same product has become ubiquitous on online markets, then it may be too difficult to distinguish the business from everyone else's, and it may no longer be a good idea to focus on selling that type of product.

Here are some tactics and tips when it comes to scoping out the competition:

Use Online Tools

While there is nothing wrong with simply looking over and exploring their website, and that is in fact the first step, in order to get a more in – depth understanding of how your competitors are doing, some online tools may be made use of. There are some site explorers such as SEMrush that allow the gathering of data such as the ranking and domain authority of a website while needing only the URL. This tool would help the retailer get a better idea of where their traffic is coming from, and how people are getting access to their website. These online tools, in conjunction with examining the website manually would give a more holistic view of how they are doing, as opposed to simply eyeballing their business.

Order their products

While this may initially seem counter – intuitive, as ordering from the competition means giving them business, ordering from competitors is a way to get valuable insights. While the general flow of ordering online tends to remain the same, there are always quirks, little things and details that distinguish one company from another, which can give an idea of what things should be avoided, or what things can be improved upon in the ordering process. Remember that in a drop shipping business, the only real interaction that a customer will have with something controlled by the retailer is the product platform and ordering process, so it's to the benefit of the retailer to make the ordering process as smooth as they can. Note that the order process should not simply be copied, but rather used as inspiration for ideas of how to make a well – oiled and smooth order process.

Analyze their social media

In the current day and age, social media is king. Perhaps not literally, but if social media can make or break a long – term established brand, what more a fledgling e – commerce drop shipping business carried out entirely in cyberspace, the same region where social media is located. Social media is one of the best ways to get feedback and to observe how people perceive the business. Watching the social media channels of competitors gives you an idea of the problems that they have, and the things that they are doing right. Picking up tips from how they engage with customers online is a way to improve one's own social media marketing methods. In addition, looking at their content is a good way to be able to find out how to compete and design a marketing strategy that would be able to overtake theirs.

How to Find the Right Drop Shipping Supplier for You

The drop shipping business model is highly reliant on the supplier; after all, it is the supplier that will be fulfilling orders, since they will provide the product and deliver it, and without the supplier there will be no business. Of course this means that the supplier is one of the most, if not the most important part of the puzzle when it comes to establishing a successful drop shipping business. If the supplier messes up a delivery, sends defective goods, or is constantly out of stock, your drop shipping business is the one that customers will blame, so it is of paramount importance that the merchant will be able to find a reliable drop shipping supplier that is capable of communicating well and fulfilling their obligations. The following are a few tips for finding a drop shipping supplier that you can trust:

Experienced Sales Representatives

Sales representatives are the first line of communication of a company, and these sales representatives are most likely those that the retailer will be working with most of the time. If these sales representatives are experienced at their job, they will most likely know how drop shipping goes, and the ins and outs of the process, allowing them to more easily handle any issues that come up and coordinate with the retailer to handle any issues that come up. An experienced sales representative will be able to put the retailer's mind at ease, as they are adept at communicating and will be able to make things move much quicker and smoother.

High quality products

Though an ecommerce store does not have the traditional brand hallmarks, it is still a brand that the retailer will wish to develop. After all, it is key to the drop shipping platform's success that the platform be recognized as a reliable place to buy high – quality products. A retailer is judged by the products that they sell and the quality of service that they provide, and the supplier handles both of those things, though the service to a lesser extent. If the supplier has high – quality products, customers will end up more satisfied, which means repeat customers and a good reputation, and good reviews and recommendations are one of the best ways to boost business and keep the retailer afloat. A reputation for selling low quality goods, on the other hand, is a quick way to sink any chance of success.

Technologically Capable

A good drop shipper keeps up with the times and is able to match the latest technological needs. Whether it be by having an inventory software that ensures that their stock availability is always up to date, or an efficient warehousing system to dispatch orders quickly, or even by simply having a well – automated order receiving system, it is important for a drop shipper to be capable. This will come in handy especially when it comes to scaling the business, in case the merchant wishes to expand, as they can feel secure that their trusted business partner will be capable of scaling along with their operations.

Punctuality and Efficiency

Drop shipping is not only about the products, but about a safe and efficient shipping system. If there is a drop shipping supplier that offers same day shipping, or at least shipping within twenty – four to forty – eight hours from receipt of the order, this will go a long way in making customers happy with the service. In a highly competitive market, any edge goes a long way, and a quick and efficient delivery system is a way to gain customers. One way of ensuring that the supplier is actually efficient with their order fulfillment process is to test them by ordering a few items, just to see how fast they are able to fulfil the order.

Where to look for Drop Shipping suppliers

If you happen to be an experienced businessman, or are friends with one, then most likely you will already have access to one or more reliable suppliers that are also capable of fulfilling drop shipping functions. However, not everyone is so lucky, and in case there are no contacts available, the best way to look for a drop shipping supplier in an area near you, funnily enough, is to simply Google it. There are many websites online, among them start – up incubators that provide directories of various drop shippers that provide various products. Once the retailer finds a few promising leads in a suitable area, it is simple to send them a quick and polite email in order to inquire about their services and a possible partnership. Sending an email over calling is preferable, as an email chain would allow you to keep a record of the conversation, as well as allow you to gauge how well and how quick their sales representatives do at replying to inquiries.

Drop Shipping fulfilment

While we have already gone over the basics of drop shipping order fulfilment, some aspects still need to be taken care of on the part of the retailer, such as whether some steps should be automated or not. Some components of the process such as the receipt of the order, the shipping information, and other such details can be automated, or can be handled manually, depending on the preference and resources available to the retailer. In case of multiple suppliers, the fulfilment process will most likely include sending the orders through email but finding the best supplier per product per order will likely rely on factors such as delivery location, shipping cost, and product availability. In this case, the retailer needs to find a way to ensure that these details are dealt with, either through using advanced software, or manually sifting through the orders to match them to the best – fit supplier.

Drop shipping Customer Support

As has been reiterated time and time again, good customer support can make or break a business. By now the reader should know that the majority of the contribution of the retailer to the customer shopping experience is in providing the platform and in providing customer support. Thus, it is in the best interest of the supplier to build and maintain the best customer support system it can in order to look good in the eyes of the customer and distinguish themselves from their other competitors.

Phone Support

One of the most classic methods of customer support is having a phone customer support system. Not only is it classic, but it is one of the quickest ways to get in touch with the customer, and it also works to the advantage of the retailer. The retailer can have an advantage when using phone support as a human conversation makes it harder for the customer to get mad, and it also makes it easier for a trained sales representative to defuse and manage the situation. It is also more immediate, and it allows customers to resolve their issues quicker, and allows the retailer to receive feedback in a more immediate manner. In a lot of countries, especially the more developed ones, the landline phone is becoming phased out, with more and more households opting not to get a phone in the first place.

A retailer can still offer phone support through applications such as Google Voice or Skype, which will allow the benefits of voice communication while still remaining relevant and allowing people without landlines to call directly. However, this will take more internet infrastructure, as it will require the platform to have a messaging system in order to inform the customer support representatives that there is a customer that wishes to call.

Email Support

The phone support is the classic method of customer support, but in reality, most of the customer support interactions will most likely be done through email, due to its convenience and accessibility. In line with this, it would be best to have domain emails set up for your website, which would grant credibility and legitimacy, as it looks quite professional and helps in establishing a brand. In addition, email support is useful for both retailer and customer as it allows them to track what steps have been taken and they can keep a record of what has happened during the interaction. One useful software for email support is the Helpscout software, specially designed for customer support functions.

Social Media Support

Given the primacy of social media in our everyday lives, a lot of customers ask questions or direct complaints at the social media pages of brands and companies even before using official, more conventional channels. This includes posts on their page or direct messages, things that are done by customers because of the convenience, and because a large amount of the time, other customers have asked similar questions on the page, and they hope to find the answers there. In line with this, having a dedicated customer support representative handling social media will help with engaging the customers even during the times that there is negative feedback. A skilled social media handler will be able to do much with the company account, and this can help with the popularity of the brand and will help with establishing good faith.

Live Chat Support

Given the dominance of internet technologies nowadays, a lot of brands are including live chat functionality in their websites and platforms, allowing customers to have nearly – immediate access to a customer support representative, and this acts as a hybrid of a phone call and email method of customer support. This is because the response is almost immediate, but there is a written record, and the customer can easily forward data such as pictures of a defective product, or a picture of the packaging, or the tracking number of their order. However, having a live chat function is difficult for a start – up with limited resources, and viable alternatives that serve a similar function are using the direct messaging services on social media platforms. However, integrated live chat support is a good option to explore if ever the retailer has the opportunity to scale up.

Chapter 7   Marketing

Once your drop shipping store goes live and it is ready to be presented to its first customers, now is the time to get it in front of as many prospective customers as you can and attract them to become paying customers. This is one of the most challenging parts of starting a drop shipping business. However, without promoting your business, your chances of success are next to zero. Luckily, if you commit yourself and do it right, you will get massive results.

You can use several channels to promote your drop shipping business. While each business has a different channel that works best for it, I am going to look at five proven methods you can use to promote your online store. You don't have to use all of them; just focus on the methods that suit you best.

Social Media Marketing (SMM)

SMM is the use of social media sites to create brand awareness, create customer relationships, gain traffic, and drive sales. These can be done on major social media platforms such as Facebook, Twitter, Instagram, Pinterest, Google+, LinkedIn, and YouTube, as well as on online forums and blogs. While many people see social media as nothing more than a social tool, it is something that you can leverage to drive sales for your drop shipping business. When you create a social media marketing campaign for your business, you should avoid trying to market your business on every social media platform. While it might seem like a good strategy to gain maximum reach, it will be overwhelming for you, and you will end up achieving dismal results on each of these sites. What you should do is identify two to three social media platforms that will deliver maximum results and completely focus on them. All in all, social media is a great tool to market your drop shipping business, so it's a big risk to avoid using this tool.

Facebook Ads

Though it is an offshoot of social media marketing, advertising on Facebook deserves its own mention due to its effectiveness as an online marketing tool. Facebook is the largest and most popular social marketing platform in the world. The platform has over 1.71 billion monthly active users, which makes it the ideal place to advertise your drop shipping business. However, the effectiveness of Facebook as a marketing tool goes beyond the numbers. Unlike most advertising platforms that serve ads on query-based data, Facebook serves its ads based on contextual data. With query-based data, the advertising platform shows adverts that are relevant to what users are searching for on the internet. A good example of a query-based advertising platform is Google Adwords.

In contrast, platforms that serve advertisements based on contextual data allow advertisers to choose the demographics of the people they want to present the ads to. This makes it easier for you to target a specific audience. Are your products geared toward 25-year-old men living in California who be obsessed with sports bikes? With Facebook ads, you can target this exact group. Facebook advertisements allow you to choose your audience based on factors like age, geographical location, interests, behavior, job position, and so much more. This means that Facebook advertisements are more relevant and are more likely to drive conversions.

To make your Facebook advertising campaign more effective, you should first come up with a clear objective for the campaign. Is your aim to create awareness for your brand? Is it to drive people to your drop shipping store? Is it to increase your sales? Having a clear objective will help you craft an effective marketing campaign. On top of that, Facebook provides you with a variety of options that make it easier for you to achieve your marketing objectives.

To create a relevant Facebook advertisement, the other things you should keep in mind is to ensure that you use persuasive, relevant, and actionable copy, relevant and attention-grabbing images, and a clear and concise Call to Action (CTA).

Search Engine Optimization (SEO)

Search Engine Optimization is the process of fine-tuning your site to capture traffic from search engines like Google. In other words, it is the process of ensuring that your drop shipping business can be found on search engines. SEO is a broad topic that consists of many elements. However, to make it simpler to understand, SEO can be broken down into steps. The first one is defining the keywords that you want your site to rank for. This means that when people search for specific keywords, they should be able to find your site on the first page of Google. You will have to do extensive keyword research to find appropriate keywords that you want to rank for. The second step is optimizing your site for the keywords you defined in step one. Step three is building backlinks to your drop shipping store. Having many backlinks on your drop shipping store gives Google's algorithms the perception that your site is an authoritative one, which in turn leads to a higher ranking on the search engine's result page.

By properly utilizing SEO tactics, your drop shipping store will rank higher on search engines, which means that more people will find your store, visit it, and buy your products. SEO allows you to direct traffic to your drop shipping store without having to pay for it.

While performing proper SEO to ensure your store ranks high on search results is not necessarily an easy task, it is still doable. Defining the keywords you want to rank for and optimizing your store for these keywords is the easy part. The hard part is trying to outrank your competitors for the same keywords, especially when your store is still relatively new and has yet to build some authority. This is where backlinks come in handy. Backlinks from high-quality sources will help raise your store's authority.

You want to ensure that you are doing SEO correctly because according to data by Custora, organic search traffic drives about 26% of all orders on e-commerce stores. By improving your site's SEO, you can increase your sales by up to 26% percent. One thing you should keep in mind is that with SEO, you won't see immediate results. Initially, you will hardly see any results, but in the long run, you will reap exponential rewards.

Email Marketing

Email is one of the most cost-effective tools you can use to market your drop shipping business and gain customer engagement. Email generates high-quality leads and high-quality conversions, which is why it has a 44% return on investment (ROI). If you do it right, you will see massive results. Email is extremely effective because people share their contact details voluntarily, which is a sure-fire sign that they are interested in your products. Email marketing also allows you to accumulate your prospect's personal data, which you can use in further interactions. By providing quality content through email, you can create more demand for your products.

To run an effective email marketing campaign, you should have an attractive lead magnet for your site. As a drop shipping business, your lead magnet can be a loyalty program that provides subscribers with exclusive discounts. You should have a well-designed email template and ensure that you regularly communicate with your subscribers. However, this does not mean constantly spamming them with sales emails, as this will only lead to people opting out of your email list. Instead, you should always strive to provide value through your email newsletters.

Video Marketing

The greatest thing about video marketing is that it makes it possible for you to create an instant connection with your audience. Posts with videos lead to more time spent on your site and increased engagement. Search engine algorithms also tend to give more importance to videos, which means that using videos will improve your ranking, increase your conversions, and have greater results on your brand awareness campaign.

The most effective way of using videos to promote your drop shipping business is to create video reviews of the products you sell in your store. These can range from amateur reviews by previous customers to professional and detailed reviews of a product's features, performance, and benefits. If you decide on using video marketing to promote your store, create a YouTube channel that matches your store design, provide information about your business on the channel, and make sure that your channel is also optimized for search engines.

Chapter 8
With Your Competitors Dealing

When you know your competitors, you have a good idea about the market standard, making it easier for you to know about the customers' expectations. Hence, if you want to survive in that particular industry you need to bring quality products and your business can stand out, eventually making your business better and sustainable. Healthy competition results in building a successful industry. You cannot stop the competition nor can you create restrictions and barriers to enter the market. However, you should learn from the strategies and policies your competitors adopt to become successful. Before implementing any plan to cope with stiff competition you should have an idea of the big dropshipping entities, how such large-scale businesses are run successfully, and what they do when they are up against competition. If you are a newcomer to dropshipping, most of the big company rules will not apply to you but that does not mean you should not take ideas from them. You can adopt and test out strategies with your store's product line and see how well they work.

Just like you, your competitors are used to following their competition and due to the internet, this has become easier than ever. You can make a list where you can keep tabs on companies that have entered the market before you, along with those which are going to be launched soon. Knowing who you are competing with helps you prepare a better plan for the battle that you are getting yourself into. Unless and until you have an extremely unique product that targets a small market, you will undoubtedly have competition. On the contrary, it will be wise to pay closer attention to the products that the other stores are selling. Do not just settle with the picture descriptions but try to analyze how they advertise, who are their distribution channels are, what their values are, and the age demographic they are targeting with their niche products. You should expect the same to happen to your store and be smart about giving out details about your products, especially when you are sharing anything on social media. Monitoring what they do and how your competitors work around certain issues will also help you make backup plans and make sure you are ready to deal with complex situations in the longer run.

Another perspective which you should adopt is to understand where your business stands and what your role is in the market. Having the ability to understand the market is a gift and can help you understand the potential of your product line. It is important to know whether the demand for a product is increasing or decreasing or remaining stable. You can make calculated decisions about how much competition you can face if you move forward with that product. If you find it too risky, try to work on finding a special niche that you feel passionate about; you can start small but grow as the market for the new product expands.

Tools For Analyzing Competitors

Google Alerts

This tool gives you well-rounded information about the industry you are involved with. You can check your status and understand where you stand through email alerts. You can receive notifications whenever your search term appears on Google. Since it is the best and the most accurate search engine available, it is highly unlikely that you will miss any notifications when your search terms appear. This is a trustworthy and reliable source of information. You can also utilize it to stay updated on your competitors and your niche. If there are any trendy niches that your industry is following, this tool is enough to get you accustomed and keep you updated.

Utilizing SEO

Having your store on the first page of a Google search is hard and requires a lot of time and effort. When you are using SEO, you should not expect instant results to have your store be on the first page of the search results. You should try out new and interesting strategies to make the most of your situation. One way could be to not use generic images that every other dropshipping business is promoting. You can re-order the products you want to sell and take photographs by yourself or use a professional photographer that is within your budget. Customization always works in your favor. Additionally, SEO helps you understand product quality and decide whether you want to be associated with this supplier or not. All these can help you reach a higher ranking in search results but in the short term, you have to rely on paid advertisements and PPC to be able to at least break even with your direct competitors.

Understanding Your Competitors

If you are thinking of getting into the competitive market of dropshipping, you need to have sound knowledge in understanding who your direct competitors are. You cannot make assumptions and design strategies around companies that you are not competing with. If you do that, you will waste your resources, funds, and be headed towards a failed business venture, not in the near future but in the long run. You need to know who they are and what prices they are quoting for the same products that your store is also selling. You should not rest after analyzing one or two competitors, it is essential for you to list all of them in your region. You should not think of offering the lowest prices; this will result in a negative impression of the type of service you offer and quality of products you are selling, especially if you are a newcomer in the industry. This should not be your first option. When you find out the prices of your competitors, try to understand the market price that has already been set by them and then put a price within that range, depending on your niche. You can offer extra support through customer service or offer bundles when you see that your business is part of a saturated market. Think and plan creatively to be able to stand out among your competitors.

Being Aware Of Competition

The dropshipping industry has seen an increasing number of competitors, among all niches. You need to have a sound knowledge of what type of policies your competitors adopt along and understand the impact of their packaging and services they are willing to offer. The best method would be to order products from your competitors and assess how their services are. If you are unaware of the competition, it will be very hard for you to pinpoint what you should do better or what you could do in a better way to sustain. This can help you improve and also gain a broader customer base. Using search engines is the most effective way and you are recommended to start with this, but you need to know what you are looking for and who you are looking for. In short, you need to dig deep and read through multiple pages. Do not move on after looking at the first page. A lot of information can be misguided. On the other hand, you could get a subscription to a legitimate directory.

WorldWideBrands is a well-renowned one where you can look for thousands of pre-screened dropshipping companies. This can help you understand and strategize region-wise. You may feel conflicted about getting this subscription as most of the directories are available online but many of those are usually of low quality and would not add much to your research. Last but not least, you can think of contacting the manufacturer - the direct source - and gain information about others who are selling the same products as you through dropshipping. Here, you can rely on getting authentic information since this manufacturer is also dealing with your products and is used to being in touch with stores with similar product lines.

How To Get Your Store To Gain More Exposure In The Market?

Everyone in today's day and age uses Google to look for products. Even if they use other search engines, the process is similar. They use keywords to look for something specific and look at the top results on the screen. Now, if you want to match up to your competitors, you need to have your store within those primary search results. Usually the links on the first page are perceived as the most reliable ones and customers find them easier to trust, regardless of if you are new or not.

Picking the right keywords

The concept of your niche needs to be precise. If asked, you should have the ability to describe your store in three words to anyone who has never heard of your store before. These words which you have come up with to define your store will act as your store keywords. The search engines try to match the keywords you have used to describe your store and niche to the search words customers are using when they are looking for any specific product. Hence, when choosing your keywords, you need to be concise but effective because these words will represent your niche and product line.

Optimizing The Website

Optimization of your website directly deals with the procedure required to optimize or design a website from scratch in order to make it rank well in search engines. This is a direct result of the keywords which you have chosen. Optimization helps you gain a higher number of visitors, leading to an increase in the number of purchases made. This is what can help you gain an advantage over your competitors as this process can help you get a much larger volume of orders from customers. In the long term, you will be able to observe the ranking of your store and how optimization has significantly contributed to its improvement. This optimization can be done on all of your pages but when done to your homepage, category pages, and product pages, the changes are more noticeable and positive results can be observed much faster.

Improving The Visibility Of Your Store On Google

Search engine optimization allows your store to gain much more exposure but it requires time. The effects of SEO last longer, but as a short-term solution, you may consider other options. PPC gives you faster and better results as the traffic in your store increases almost instantly. You can look through the websites of your competitors and find out what they are doing that you have not done yet. You can learn through this and choose the correct keywords, which in turn helps Google to attract more customers to your store. Try to be aware of strategies and techniques already adopted by your competitors.

Providing a user-friendly interface

No matter how many luxurious products your store has, if customers are unable to navigate through your store, those products will never be able to sell. When you are setting up your theme or designing your store, you should keep this in mind. Keeping in mind the idea of your product line and the age group of your targeted customers, try to choose templates and colors that fit; this will help to grab their attention for a longer period of time. Make sure the font sizes you are using are clear and that they can find where the products are, where your contact information is, where the search bar is, and so on. If they cannot navigate through your site, the whole process will be more time-consuming for them and they might prefer to make purchases elsewhere.

Providing limited-time offers

You can introduce deals on your products when you want to drive away traffic from your competitors and also during special occasions. You can set deadlines and make customers aware of the limited time offers. They can also be informed through the use of the "Recent Sales Pop-Up Plugin" that lets them know about other shoppers that have bought products with this limited time offer. They will be interested to look around for what is available for purchase as you have already ingrained the idea of purchasing in their minds. They will see an array of products that they have never explored before. Meanwhile, other customers have been targeted the same way and are making purchases simultaneously. This cycle can be continued throughout the entire time of the limited offer and the increase in activity on your site will keep on attracting more and more customers.

Promoting Upsell

Upsell is a sales technique through which the customers are induced by the seller to make more expensive purchases or upgrades in order to make a higher percentage of profit per sale. This strategy is by far one of the most effective ones when you want your customers' attention. When they are sure about what they are looking for, they can add the product keywords in your search bar. When they are provided with the list of items, they are also presented with an extended product range. You need to put in a bit of work here beforehand. For every product that your store displays, you should have another additional list of products that your customers can access. They will make the customers feel like your store is a one-stop shop and that they do not need to look around at other stores. They will spend a more significant amount of time on your website browsing and looking for desired products and also for complementary products they may want to purchase. Upsell surely enhances your profits.

Having unique content

You should always be on the lookout for new niches that are still untouched. You can start by sorting out what your competitors do not have and this will help you stand out. When you have items that are not available on any other stores, it will be comparatively easier for you to drive traffic to your store. As long as your store is the only one, you can charge high prices as if it is something that the customers have always needed but could not find, they will be ready to pay high prices. However, when you see that other competitors have also introduced this niche, you can regulate prices according to theirs. Availability of an alternative should not worry you since you were the first to introduce the product and customers have purchased from you before. Hence, this sense of security will enable them to keep coming back to you even if your competitors offer the same price.

Using videos for promotion and branding

A lot of other stores like you may not think of making videos or doing live sessions on social media platforms, thus, you can now provide that to your customers where you can directly communicate with them when they comment or inbox you with any queries. Of course, they can get the details of the product from the description but for example, how it fits, if it is a shirt or a pair of sunglasses, cannot be known simply by the pictures. This is your opportunity to represent your product line in a creative and unique way. You can develop an interactive relationship with your customer base and let them be more involved. You can also to product reviews to make them more aware. This will allow for healthy competition to thrive and also help the customers to identify your store as a top store.

Having active collaborations

You need to have faith in your niche and product line and be able to try out new ways to attract customers. When you are first starting out, it is obvious that big brands will not be willing to collaborate with you, but never forget the power of your local community. Depending upon your niche, look around for influencers and bloggers who would be interested to be associated with your store. However, you have to remember that you need to collaborate with people that are not your direct competitors. If you have a clothing store, seek out makeup artists and hairdressers and brainstorm together to get mutual benefit.

Lastly, try to think of your competitors as your friends because they can be your best teachers. Each business and product line is different. You need to be conscious of that and you should try to research as many dropshipping stores as possible.The more you are aware of your competitors, the more opportunities you will get to provide better services and explore new and unique products.

The policies adopted for certain niches will not be the same but if they can be merged into your product line or have similar target customers, you can do tests and strategize accordingly.

Chapter 9

Establishing Your Brand Through A Marketing Plan

Once you have established your supply chain and your website is up and running, it will be time to establish your brand. You do this by developing a smart marketing plan and scaling that plan to fit your estimated growth rates. The last thing you want is to create a great marketing strategy only to end up overwhelmed. That can cause you, and your business, to crash.

Scaling Up Your Business

At this point, you definitely want to know what scaling is so you feel like less of a newbie.

Scaling means that you are creating new revenue at a much faster rate than you are increasing your costs. If your costs increase with every single new income stream, then you are not really becoming profitable.

Smart business owners want to scale their business just as much as they want to grow their business. To do this, you need to have the foresight to look ahead. Scaling is tied directly to your marketing plan. Your marketing plan should give you a good idea of how fast you could grow and what you will need to have optimized to ensure your business continues to grow in profitability without picking up just as many expenses.

The primary goal here is not to eliminate costs because frankly, that is impossible. No matter how you look at it, every business has costs and overhead. What you are trying to do here is to make sure that your business has more profit than costs. You also want to be careful that you aren't working so hard for so little that the business is no longer worth it for you.

In order to do that, you will need to create a system that helps you deliver your products in services in an efficient way that can be replicated and used over and over again for little cost. This will tie into your supply chain and website. Your supply chain needs to be able to keep up with order demands. If it can't, you need a new one. Your website needs to be optimized for high volume traffic. Things as simple as you create an easier system for payment can help scale your business.

Although scaling is important, and it is a key piece to the puzzle that is a successful business, you need to strategize and scale proportionately to the business itself.

To scale to quickly could be as detrimental as not scaling, or scaling too slowly. If you are only bringing in one thousand dollars a month, you aren't going to spend five thousand dollars on scaling your operations for those sales. That is a fast way to spend too much money too quickly.

What it comes down to, essentially, is that scaling allows you to run your business efficiently and smoothly. If scaled properly, there will be no need for you to be working twenty hours a day to problem solve.

You will be able to trust that your website is running smoothly and efficiently. You will know that the ads you have in place are bringing in a steady stream of customers. Those customers will be happy because you have ensured that your supply chain could handle the growth in sales.

That is the point of scaling. It makes your life easier, and your business runs smoothly. Without scaling you would end up frustrated and overworked. Your customers would become unhappy. You may end up with a lot of growth but you will not be able to sustain it because the business is not scaled to serve that many people.

Scaling vs Growing

Growth is when your business is creating new business, but also incurring costs to match. You are bringing in customers, you are making sales, and you can see clearly that your business is increasing in size.

Whereas you used to only need to check-in and see how your store was doing once a day, you are now fielding questions and putting out fires all day long. Here is the problem: in order to see this growth you have probably spent a great deal of time and money on trying to market these products.

In the Drop shipping world, you are not making or dealing directly with the products, which is already helping you to scale. However, you still need to market and your products which will require a lot of work and a lot of money. You also need to get the orders, check that the orders are correct in your system, and get the orders to your supplier. Then, you need to be able to trust that your supplier is shipping out the products as promised when promised, and with the quality promised.

You have already read how a good, solid supply chain is one of the most important aspects of your business, but as it relates to growth and scaling there are some considerations to take a second look at.

You also need to look at how you communicate orders to your supplier.

If you are experiencing high growth and gaining customers quickly but your supplier can't deliver that quickly, you could end up losing money.

Let's say you gain one hundred new customers in less than a week and they generate you another one thousand dollars. So now it is two weeks later. Fifty of your customers got their products with no problems. They got everything on time and with no defects. You don't need to worry about those customers.

The other fifty did not have the same luck. Some products may have been late or not shipped. Maybe you missed ten of them because you have not scaled or optimized the part of your business that involves sending orders to the supplier. So you refund them.

Twenty got defective products. The other twenty got the wrong product altogether. Either way, you just lost five hundred dollars, or more, because you now need to refund or replace the items.

Had you scaled, the results would be different. You would have had an ordering system in place that automated the orders and you would not have missed that first ten.

That same system would record exactly what the customer typed and/or clicked on so you are no longer attempting to manually order everything. In addition, you would have a reliable supplier who can handle large orders so the customers would have gotten the correct items.

You may still end up with a few whose items were damaged in transit, but those customers would only make up a small percentage.

Scaling Business Culture

No matter what type of business you are running company culture is important. It sets the tone for how you and your employees treat customers, vendors, and each other. Having a company culture that involves respect, kindness, and putting the customers first can make the difference between your company thriving or failing.

Company culture starts with you. What do you want the culture to look like? How do you want the employees to treat each other? How do you want them to treat customers?

Let's say you want the culture to center around respect for employees and customers. You also want your employees to be driven and innovative. That is your culture. That is what you include when you are training new employees.

This may seem simple. Drop shipping companies usually start with just one person starting their business. However, you will eventually need employees to help with customer service and marketing at the very least. You may need more than that. The first few employees may be easy to train.

It is easy to take one or two people and say hey, this is the culture. This is what I mean. This is what I want. It will not be so easy with twenty employees. It will be even harder with fifty.

So how can you maintain your companies culture and reinforce it? How do you ensure that your employees continue providing quality customer service? How do you ensure that the employee morale stays high and you don't end up with a high turnover rate or terrible customer service?

You are the key here.

The first thing to remember is that this is your company. You need to model these behaviors. Anytime you are around your employees or talking to a customer you need to demonstrate the same qualities you are asking for. Be patient. Listen to the customer. Speak to them kindly and do all you can to resolve their issue. This shows your employees that you are not only asking them to show customers respect and kindness but that you are willing to practice what you preach.

There are many other things you can do. No one thing is enough. Make sure your managers are on board. They deal with the rest of the employees more than you do, and the more employees you have the more managers you will need. Always model this behavior to them, and talk to them about doing the same thing.

Reward employees who show the qualities you are looking for. Did Jennifer in your customer service department handle a particularly rude customer very respectfully and kindly even though you could tell she was stressed? Tell her what a great job she did. Let her take a break. Occasionally have company-sponsored luncheons or parties to thank your team.

You can also put posters and graphics around the office, and set up learning materials through the employee portal. Make the company culture a priority. Happy and cohesive groups work better and more productively than groups who feel ignored and unappreciated.

Things to Look At When Scaling Your Business

There is no shortage of considerations when you are trying to decide on what to look at to scale your business. There are so many moving parts to any Drop shipping business.

It may seem simpler than a traditional business, and in some ways it is, but in some ways it actually much more complicated since you do not control the products or shipping yourself.

The first thing you need to look at is your marketing plan and your projected growth. Assume that your business with double within a month. Could you handle that? If all of your projections have you making two hundred orders a day within the next two months, how would you handle that?

Let's start with the basics.

Are you using a quality website platform? Have you ensured that your platform, in particular, has shown that it does not crash with heavy traffic? Is it fast enough?

On average, if a website takes more than two to four seconds to load, almost a quarter of the potential customers would leave the site. You need to have a high-quality provider to guarantee your site can handle heavy traffic and fast load times.

How are the payments being processed? Do you offer enough options? Do you accept all major credit cards and payment apps? The more payment types available to your customers the more likely they are to buy.

If person A only uses PayPal for online shopping and you do not have a PayPal option then you just lost a customer.

Once you have the orders and payments, how are you communicating those orders to your supplier? Do you have an automated system in place?

Having a close working relationship with your dropshipper is always the best way to handle things like this. That way, if you choose to make life easier by automating your system, you can still make sure that if there are any issues you will know about it right away.

Do all of your systems work well together? If you have an automated payment system, an automatic ordering system, and systems controlling your bookkeeping and more, do they "speak" to each other? The more automated all of your systems are and the more they can share information with each other the better.

Finally, let's talk about employees.

Will you need more? Having a tech on call is a good idea, of course. What about an assistant? Maybe someone who is more experienced in marketing? Remember, you want to scale, not just grow.

Hire who you need to for business to run smoothly, but not before you need them, and automate as much as you can so that you only need a few employees.

For example, if you are up to a thousand orders per week, you can have three employees. One tech, one marketing expert, and someone that helps you to field customer calls. Your automated systems handle the rest.

How to Scale Your Drop shipping Business

So far you have learned what scaling is and why it is important. Now you can learn what you can do to scale your Drop shipping business in a way that makes sense and works for you.

Let's assume you have already gone over all of the details in the "Things to Look at When Scaling Your Business" section. So now you want to know what to do once you have evaluated your business and looked into all of the different things you could streamline.

Start by once again combing through your marketing plan and your current growth rate. How many new customers and new sales can you expect for the next month? How about for the next six months? How about for the next year? Project your growth, and work backward from there.

Do not hire four employees to take customer calls when you won't have more than a hundred orders in an entire week. It is unlikely every customer would call, and even if they did, one employee could handle one hundred calls in a week.

Talk to your suppliers. This can not be said enough. Your Drop shipping partner is the person who supplies all of your customers with the products. They keep the stock, they take the orders from you, and they pack and ship all of your orders.

You can have every perfected system in place. You could have the absolute best advertising and the most amazing website. The entire business will fail if you do not communicate with your suppliers.

Let them know what the projected growth rate is. Make sure they know how much inventory you think they may need. Let them know that orders will be increasing so they can decide if they need to add people to their team to keep up.

Also, attempt to make your costs lower. If you are reaching a certain benchmark, try to talk to them about taking off a percentage for so many bulk orders.

Get a freelancer or hire a techie who is experienced in building entire business systems. You need someone who can optimize your website. They should also be able to set up your payment systems, your ordering systems, your phone systems, your bookkeeping software and more.

Get a professional who can automate as much as they can and then tie it all together so they work well together. Keep that person on retainer in case anything goes down. This person will be invaluable. The right systems save you time, money, and stress.

Speaking of money, pay attention to your accounts! Some banks and payment apps will flag and block funds if they feel something is fraudulent. They don't necessarily know you are running a business. Communicating with them and heading off any problems before they start can go a long way in preventing any accounts from being frozen or blocked.

As your business grows you will need to hire customer service representatives. You cannot spend twenty-four hours a day awake and taking calls and responding to emails.

It is important to deal with customers, but you are a busy person and no matter how much you'd like to, you can't take fifty calls and a hundred emails in a day by yourself on top of running everything else.

Hire an assistant to help you manage all of this. Have someone responsible you can trust working directly with you to help with anything you need. They should be able to do anything from grabbing you a coffee to handling calls to your supplier if you need them to.

Throughout all of this, treat everyone who works for you well and always do your best to model the company culture you want to create.

Why a Marketing Plan is Essential when Scaling Your Business

Your marketing plan is probably the most important part of your overall business planning. It outlines your products, how you plan to market these products, and who you are marketing to.

The marketing plan is your go-to when trying to make decisions in your scaling operations.

Your marketing plan is created based on data. You will have done research and looked into every single detail of your business and projected growth. This data will then be compiled and analyzed at which point you will put it all together in a cohesive way.

It will include your overall plan along with sections outlining how much money you plan to make, how you plan to make it, and when you plan to make. Your goals will be set and you will have data to support your projected goals.

When scaling your business your market plan will be your most important tool. This will be your guide. It will give you a clear timeline. Scaling is a process. It is not something that you can do overnight. You need to make strategic changes and decisions based on your marketing plan's projected goals and timelines.

For example, if you have planned and projected that at three months you want your website to have two hundred and fifty thousand visitors a month then you will need to scale to meet that goal. Which means you will need to scale your advertising. You could choose to hire someone for that goal.

You can use sites such as Upwork and Fiverr to find freelancers to write your copy for you and create social media content, or you can choose to do it yourself.

In the meantime, if you have grown your website traffic by that much you will have also built your sales way up. This means you should also ensure that by that three-month mark you have also set up all of your payment and ordering systems so that the process is streamlined for you, your customers, and your dropshipper.

You would have hired a programmer to set all of that up for you and a customer service rep to help you handle any incoming customer problems.

Throughout all of this, you would have talked to your Drop shipping partner about the projected increase in product needs. That way you could make sure they can handle the influx on their end as well.

This is just an example of why a marketing plan is essential to building your business. Because for each milestone you have outlined in your plan you can already have a solid way to ensure you hit it by properly scaling in accordance.

If you do not use a marketing plan, your company may grow, but you will not have planned out how to grow all of the moving parts with it. So how do you create this all-important marketing plan?

Creating a Great Marketing Plan

A marketing plan can be time-consuming to create, but it can save you time and thousands of dollars down the line. The very first thing you need to do is sit down and detail where you are now and decide what your goals are and why you chose those as your goals.

Remember to keep these goals clear and concise because later you will need to flesh it all out. You also need to have the data to work with, such as what types of ads and content attract the demographic you are targeting.

For example, you would not write "gain a million twitter followers". This is vague and not based on any type of data set. You would write "gain a million twitter followers by hiring an experienced writer to write articles specific to "my niche" and targeted customer demographics. I will post three articles per day every day, and ensure the writer uses set keywords in the articles. I will gain one hundred thousand followers every two weeks until I hit a million"

Customer demographics will be a large part of your overall marketing strategy, so you want to include as much about them as you can. Do as much research as you can possibly afford to do when studying these demographics.

If you are selling gaming headphones, for example, you would need to do studies and research to determine the people most likely to buy them. Let's say that the research shows that these headphones will primarily sell to young males between the ages of sixteen and twenty-five.

You need to know all you can about males between sixteen and twenty-five in order to cater all of your marketing content to them. Targeted marketing works better than any general marketing you could do.

Now that you have your current standing and goals outlined, your timeline, and your scaling strategy to match, you can fill in the rest of your marketing strategy. Include demographic details.

Write a solid but to the point executive summary outlining who you are and what type of values you want your company to represent. Research your competitors and find out what works and doesn't work for them.

Outline your overall marketing strategies and how you plan to track all of your growth and changes so you can continue to scale in advance.

Ultimately, your marketing plan should be clear, concise, and informative. Make it attractive to look at so anyone who needs to see it wants to read it. Keep your executive summary to the point while still giving the reader a clear idea of what you want to convey. Make your goals and the plan of execution to those goals clear and detailed. Make sure the reader can clearly see who your targeted audience will be, and how you will keep track of all of your progress.

This marketing plan will be your guide. You will refer to it to make any changes necessary to scale your business. You will refer to it when talking to any investors or at any meetings with other business owners. You will use it to inform your employees about the overall strategy and goals of the company and what you need from them.

This plan will be something you look back and follow for years to come, and a good marketing plan will cover ten years or more. You can always go in and adjust it based on new data.

Most importantly, this marketing plan is what will help you securely establish your brand in a strategic way.

Conclusion

As you begin working your drop shipping business, you are going to begin to learn your own tips and tricks to help you master the business. However, to help you get started, we have compiled a list of some of the best tips and tricks you should pay attention to when you are starting your drop shipping business. Having this knowledge under your belt now and applying them immediately will ensure that you are prepared for everything that is to come and that you come out of the gates strong.

It is a good idea to keep a book handy so that as you learn your own tips and tricks in the industry, you can write them down. While you may remember some due to using them on a regular basis, having them written down can help you remember what works in the situations you don't tend to experience as often, such as specific situations with certain vendors. Make sure that you keep this notebook handy and that you use it whenever you need in order to make sure that you are running your business smoothly and efficiently.

As with any business, your reputation is highly important. You need to recognize what goes into creating a solid reputation and how you can use your reputation to positively impact your business performance. Your reputation is closely attached to your brand, but it is not your brand itself. Instead, it is the way people think about your brand.

Take a moment to think about a company that you haven't had such a good experience with. It is likely that many people haven't had a good experience, and for you and the rest of the population, their reputation is tarnished. People may continue to shop there, but it does not equate to them gaining as much business as they could if they had a positive reputation.

Now, think about a business that you love shopping with. Think about how positive they make you feel and the type of experience you have when you do business with them. Also, think about how other people tend to talk about that business. Since their overall reputation is more positive and they are known to serve their customers effectively, it is likely that their reputation is excellent.

With your own business, you want to be the one with the reputation that has people eager to work with you. People should be aware of how positive your business is and the type of experience they can expect to have with you well before the first time they ever do business with you. When people run into issues with their service, they should be able to rely on the fact that your company will rectify the situation quickly and in a justified manner. The customer needs to know that you are always going to look out for their best interest and do everything you can to serve them to the highest of your abilities.

www.ingramcontent.com/pod-product-compliance
Lightning Source LLC
Chambersburg PA
CBHW070628220526
45466CB00001B/125